TEN
of shades
GREEN

ARCHITECTURE AND THE NATURAL WORLD

PETER BUCHANAN

The Architectural League of New York

PUBLISHED BY

The Architectural League of New York

457 Madison Avenue

New York, NY 10022

212 753 1722

www.archleague.org

DISTRIBUTED BY

W. W. Norton & Company, Inc.

500 Fifth Avenue

New York, NY 10110

www.wwnorton.com

W.W. Norton & Company Ltd.

Castle House

75/76 Wells Street

London WIT 3QT

Major support for the exhibition *Ten Shades of Green* was provided by
the Lily Auchincloss Foundation, Inc. Additional support was provided by public
funds from the National Endowment for the Arts and the New York State
Council on the Arts, a state agency. Support was also provided by the Norman
and Rosita Winston Foundation; the Department of State Development,
Queensland Government, Australia; the Graham Foundation for Advanced
Studies in the Fine Arts; the J. Clawson Mills Fund; and the Vinmont Foundation.

The national tour of *Ten Shades of Green* was made possible by contributions
from Perkins & Will, a national architecture firm, and Herman Miller.

This book was made possible by a contribution from the LEF Foundation.

Design by Asya Palatova

Library of Congress Cataloging-in-Publication Data

Buchanan, Peter.

Ten shades of green : architecture and the natural world / Peter Buchanan.—1st ed.

    p. cm.

Includes bibliographical references.

ISBN 0-393-73189-8 (pbk.)

1. Architecture—Environmental aspects. 2. Sustainable architecture. I. Title.

II. Title: 10 shades of green. II. Architectural League of New York.

NA2542.35.B83 2005

720'.47—dc22

              2005014411

Preface *by Rosalie Genevro*

THIS BOOK DOCUMENTS THE EXHIBITION *Ten Shades of Green*, organized by the Architectural League, with Peter Buchanan as curator, and launched in New York in the spring of 2000. The League's goal with *Ten Shades* was straightforward: to show examples of work that combined environmental responsibility with formal ambition. Peter Buchanan accomplished that goal, beautifully, in the projects he chose and described, which range widely both in formal composition and in the ways in which they engage environmental issues. He also created something larger: a context for understanding those projects, and for evaluating all works of architecture and land planning, that embraces a range of concerns from technical efficiency to communal well-being to emotional resonance. *Ten Shades of Green* struck a chord, and the exhibition traveled to galleries and museums all over the United States from 2000 through the end of 2004, propelled by word of mouth of architects who had seen it and wanted to bring it to their own cities and institutions as a way to educate and move their communities forward.

At the time the exhibition opened in New York, and that Peter Buchanan's essay in this book was written, the current cycle of environmentalism in American architecture was just coming into focus. The United States Green Building Council, a consortium of building industry companies, firms, and individuals, had been formed in 1993 and launched the first public version of its LEED (Leadership in Energy and Environmental Design) standards in 2000. Four Times Square, a skyscraper by Fox and Fowle Architects and one of the most publicized early works of a new generation of green buildings, opened in New York in 1999. Members of the American Institute of Architects formed the first chapter of the Committee on the Environment in the mid 90s.

Since then there has been a great deal of activity and progress in the relationship of American architecture to environmental issues. A large number of architects have begun to embrace the basics of environmentally responsible design, and there is much talk among architects and their clients about LEED certification, about gaining the technical proficiency to achieve LEED "silver" or "gold" or "platinum" buildings. No large firm, or small firm for that matter, can afford not to market their "green" capabilities as they seek commissions. Public and institutional clients from the federal General Services Administration to cities and universities around the country have made creation of "green guidelines" a priority in their building and infrastructure development programs. The spring of 2005 brought the news that the mayors of 132 American cities have pledged to meet the Kyoto goals of reducing greenhouse gas emissions by 7% from 1990 levels by 2012. A number of the design leaders of the profession have taken on sustainable design as a conscious determinant of form in their work, in buildings such as recent Pritzker Prize winner Thom Mayne's CalTrans headquarters in Los Angeles and San Francisco Federal Building. A few influential developers have made environmental responsibility a priority in their projects, and have sought out architects who can meet their ambitions.

But it is sobering to reflect on the larger context within which this progress has taken place, to confront how little, fundamentally, has changed, and how much, and with what intense urgency, needs to. Our global predicament is clear to those who care to pay attention. A number of recent publications—ranging from Jared Diamond's magisterial *Collapse*, documenting the failures of societies that have failed to act as responsible environmental stewards, to a recent United Nations report showing how the squandering of natural capital is dramatically affecting economic well-being—lay out in stark terms the consequences of irresponsibility.[1] Yet in the United States, overall environmental progress is stalled, if not moving backward. Daily fuel consumption to power our cars has risen from 5.1 million barrels in 1970 to 8.3 million in 2002; cars are as heavy, again, as they were in the 1970s, the number of vehicles has exploded and the average number of miles driven per vehicle has risen dramatically.[2] The development of suburban and exurban land continues, in patterns that demand continuing use of huge amounts of energy, while the enormous investments sunk long ago in the fabric of many cities in the Northeast and Midwest go wasted. Americans seem to be voting, with their ballots, their wallets, and their feet, as if environmental problems either don't exist or are someone else's concern.

What can architects do in the face of this immense challenge?

In the fall of 2004, an article called "The Death of Environmentalism" roiled the environmental movement. The authors, Michael Schnellenberger and Ted Nordhaus, charge that mainstream environmentalists have become so focused on narrow technical and regulatory strategies that they have forsaken two critical tasks: fully and persuasively imagining a better world, and reaching across the boundaries of specific interests to build coalitions. Both, the authors argued, are necessary if a broad-based, powerful, energized movement is to be built that can move society to effective action on global warming, looming water shortages, other resource depletion, and species extinction.[3]

American architecture is in a parallel situation. American environmentalism in architecture, to date, has been largely focused on technical fixes, on figuring out how to build essentially the same buildings that have always been built, but to make them consume less energy. The profession is on its way to mastering the technical skills needed to improve the how of building, certainly an important step forward; but it has not taken on, nor asked its clients to take on, the bigger questions of what is to be built, and

why. We won't get where we need to go, in environmental terms, if we focus on narrowly technical questions and never confront, in a profound way, the cultural attitudes and appetites that have brought us to where we are. Technical mastery is necessary, but not sufficient. "Sustainability," as Wilfried Wang has written, "is a cultural problem."[4]

What architects can offer, what they must offer, are visions of fundamentally new arrangements for new ways of life. Architects must take on the big questions of land use patterns and transportation and space standards and hyperconsumption and waste, and challenge themselves to create positive visions of ways of living that protect the planet and still offer opportunity and comfort. Utopia, of course, has been in disrepute as an architectural project for quite some time, for good historical reasons. What is needed now is a new sort of utopian thinking: not utopia as set-piece, but interrelated and far-reaching visions for the built future that can be tested, discussed, rejected, improved, and embraced as part of a society-wide discussion. Specifically skilled as they are at understanding, influencing, imagining, and creating physical frames for ways that people want to live, architects can contribute ideas and forms to make visible the possibilities of a reinvention of our way of life. That reinvention, as Peter Buchanan rightly argues in this book, is the great creative challenge of contemporary culture.

1
Jared Diamond, *Collapse: How Societies Choose to Fail or Succeed* (New York: Viking, 2004); Andrew Revkin, "Report Tallies Hidden Cost of Human Assault on Nature," *The New York Times* (April 5, 2005, Section F, page 2).
2
Worldwatch Institute, *Vital Signs 2005: The Trends that are Shaping Our Future* (New York: W.W. Norton & Company, 2005), p. 56.
3
Michael Shellenberger and Ted Nordhaus, "The Death of Environmentalism: Global Warming Politics in a Post-Environmental World," 2004, www.thebreakthrough.org
4
Wilfried Wang, "Sustainability is a Cultural Problem," *Harvard Design Magazine* (No. 18, Spring/Summer 2003).

Foreword *by Kenneth Frampton*

AS THE TWENTY-FIRST CENTURY OPENS TO AN increasingly globalized future, the ethic of sustainability comes to the fore as a compelling principle for the revitalization of architecture and for the mediation of the entropic conditions currently obtaining between the drive towards economic maximization and the fragility of the natural environment. The excessive production of carbon dioxide, leading to the so-called greenhouse effect, and the concomitant phenomena of global warming are surely among the more traumatic transformations that have accompanied our entry into an epoch that is challenged by other equally intractable contradictions, above all, perhaps, our capacity for the digital control of every conceivable process while remaining incapable of containing pollution, along with our excessive production of commodities and our ever escalating maldistribution of wealth. Although the practice of architecture alone cannot be expected to affect an aporetic condition of such overwhelming magnitude, it has nonetheless become evident that the development of a more symbiotically responsive approach towards the design of the built environment can only have a fundamentally beneficial effect upon the quality of life that it necessarily helps to engender.

While we already know that 5% of the world's population— namely the current population of the United States— consumes some 20% of the world's resources, we are generally less aware that the built environment as a whole is responsible for at least half of this annual consumption of energy, as opposed to the 30% which we seemingly expend on transportation modes of various kinds. It is this statistic that brings home more forcibly than any other comparative figure the need for the cultivation of a more nuanced, symbiotic approach towards the design of the built form.

By virtue of positing ten fundamental principles and then documenting, in parallel, an equal number of exemplary buildings, Peter Buchanan's remarkably didactic and comprehensive exhibition, *Ten Shades of Green*, inaugurated at the Architectural League of New York in 2000 and which has since traveled extensively around the United States, has done much to raise our consciousness of the full ramifications of this issue. One can hardly endorse enough the paradoxical point with which Buchanan opens his polemic, namely, his crucial insistence that there is no such thing as a green architecture or a green aesthetic and that sustainability in architecture arises out of a subtle, often imperceptible interaction between built form and the ambient forces that impinge upon its surface. What one seeks under this rubric then is a nature/culture interplay in the deepest possible sense. Thus one looks to establish a continuous feedback modification, not only with respect to the one-off building but also with regard to the discipline as a whole. Needless to say, it is exactly at this juncture that the issue of sustainability begins to confront many of our more cherished prejudices with regard to the nature of architectural practice and with this, by implication, the current scope and mandate of architectural education. One encroaches here on the hallowed ground of our so-called creative freedom and it may well be that nothing less than a frontal assault, such as Buchanan's thesis, will ever establish an effective inroad into the aestheticized stronghold of architectural academia, not to mention the spectacular modes of practice that it largely serves to legitimize. As Susannah Hagan has put it of what we might call our received modes of education and practice:

> An enormous gulf exists between those who look to a new model of nature as the source of new generative strategies and/or forms and those who look to it as the source of new ways of constructing and running buildings. The intellectual pyrotechnics of the former are missing in the latter. The intellectual consistency of the latter is missing in the former. Reading Thomas

Herzog and Glenn Murcutt isn't remotely as stimulating as reading Kwinter and Lynn, but reading their buildings can be. The provocation of environmental practitioners lies in what their buildings are doing, not in their discussion of it.[1]

Surely the divide to which she alludes stems in the last analysis from the difference between, on the one hand, the subjective belief that genuine tectonic creativity is solely dependent on arbitrary forms of individual expression, however much these may be scientifically adduced, and, on the other, the conviction that it must, on the contrary, be grounded in the deeper cause of more restricted creativity that is contingent on our collective cultivation of a material culture: one that is not only ecologically grounded but also, at times, as self-effacing in its precepts as it is ethically and critically consistent.

Buchanan's ten exemplary sustainable structures cover a wide range of both technical means and environmental forms, passing from such high-tech, high performance, energy-conserving structures, as Norman Foster's Commerzbank, Frankfurt of 1997 to such low-tech, low-cost assemblies as Lindsay and Kerry Clare's Cotton Tree experimental housing realized in 1994 under the auspices of the Queensland government on Australia's Sunshine Coast. It is significant that Buchanan's assessment of this last passes from an appraisal of its socio-cultural structure to a discussion of its more delicate interstitial elements as though they are both part and parcel of the same ecologically sensitive approach, where the built "ecosystem" is to be seen as an artificial interface with nature.

In his more generically theoretical discourse Buchanan shows us how "green" buildings may be used to conserve and recycle water in various ways from the harvesting of rainwater in storage tanks to the filtering of "gray water" from baths and basins so that this water may be reused to flush toilets, after it has been filtered through reed beds. The fact that such beds may be used to integrate a building into its surrounding landscape touches once again, as we have already noted, on the wider socio-cultural dimensions of the sustainable approach. Buchanan continually draws our attention to the critical role to be played by topography in the future development of architectural culture, particularly as this may be brought to mediate the universal placelessness of the megalopolis. Hence the imperative to inlay form with the ground, for it is increasingly evident that given our entropic motopian environment we hardly need to indulge in the further proliferation of free-standing objects, irrespective of their aesthetic merit. Under point seven of his decalogue, treating with the rubric of place, Buchanan evokes the crucial role to be played by the topographic in all its aspects when he refers to the computer's capacity to synthesize and model the microclimate that surrounds a given building. By such an agency we may come to terms, in a more effective way, with the ecology, geology and hydrology of the given context, so as to minimize as far as possible the potentially destructive environmental impact of the new intervention.

Like the distinguished environmental engineer Michelle Addington, Buchanan reminds us that artificial illumination represents the biggest consumption of energy in built-form, followed by air-conditioning as a close second. Such excessively wasteful practices lead him to recommend shallow plan-forms on two counts, first because they reduce the need for artificial light and second because, under temperate conditions, they allow one to modify the interior climate through manually operated windows: a provision that is even mandated by law in certain European countries. Hence, his parallel advocacy of energy-saving, large, double-glazed openings that, while fully exposed to low-angle sun in winter, would remain

1
Susannah Hagen, "Five Reasons to Adopt Environmental Design," *Harvard Design Magazine*, No. 18, Spring/Summer, 2003

shielded by canopies or exterior blinds from the impact of radiant heat in summer.

This returns us to the passive hybrid environmental approach that is latent in a great deal of vernacular building. I have in mind time-honored orientational preferences in certain regions or the habitual provision of overhangs, or even the availability of thermal mass so that through the manipulation of vents, shutters and sliding screens, one is able to maintain optimal conditions irrespective of the season. One may add here, with regard to the lightweight membranes of hi-tech structures how servo-mechanisms, activated by sensors, may be discreetly employed so as to compensate for fluctuating discrepancies between the internal and the external climate.

Buchanan remains well aware that not all of his recommended principles are compatible with what Catherine Slessor has characterized as "eco-tech" structures. This is because sophisticated hi-tech designs invariably tend to ignore, almost by definition, two time-honored attributes; first, the issue of embodied energy which is all but spontaneously incorporated in vernacular building and second, the virtually unquantifiable precept of "long life, loose fit," which is all but impossible to attain in contemporary building practice. As he puts it, "green" buildings should ideally be generically adaptable and convivial rather than utilitarian and, moreover, relatively timeless rather than encumbered with gratuitous formal gestures that soon become dated. Above all they should be made of low energy materials that mellow with age, such as wood or brick, rather than with high energy synthetic substances that are often unable to withstand the long-term effects of weathering without continual maintenance.

Notwithstanding all of the above it is the application of the sustainable paradigm at an urban scale that is destined to be the critical fulcrum in the long haul, for as Buchanan points out transport and above all the automobile is the most prodigious consumer of energy after the built environment itself. And here, of course, one may well question the point of energy-efficient structures if universal commutation by car continues to prevail throughout the megalopolis, with all the deleterious environmental consequences that this invariably entails, short of shifting to hydrogen fuel cells or other forms of non-polluting propulsion.

Apart from the urgent need to find a substitute for gasoline, relatively dense residential settlement and public transport posit themselves as two interrelated strategies capable of containing the ecological footprint of the città diffusa. Everything turns in the last analysis on the pattern of future land settlement. As long as the essential social services remain disaggregated and as long as there is no complementary economic means of accessing them by public transport, then the socio-cultural, sustainable potential of the residential fabric will remain essentially underdeveloped. Buchanan is surely aware of the socially catalytic aspects of sustainable design when he writes:

> A major element of green architecture should be not just to work with and be gentle to nature, but also to make conspicuously visible its workings and cycles. This will educate people about and make them more sensitive to nature, and also give them a sense of connection with and rootedness in nature. The ultimate ideal would be an architecture that fostered in various ways a deep sense of communion with nature and the cosmos. Such an architecture is not only good for the planet, it is also the only one in which people can flower into their full potential, discovering themselves in interaction with others and opening into contact with the most ennobling of human sensibilities as they experience their connections with the larger scheme of things, and the ways in which this unfolds from past into the future. (p. 37)

As Reyner Banham instructed us over thirty years ago in his seminal book *The Architecture of the Well Tempered Environment* of 1969, none of this is entirely new, as we may well judge from Frank Lloyd Wright's fully air-conditioned Larkin Building of 1906, not to mention his equally "well-tempered" Robie House of 1909. Banham's study should surely have long since been a mandatory primer in all architectural schools, along with Ian McHarg's pioneering *Design With Nature* (1969) and John Tilman Lyle's more current *Regenerative Design for Sustainable Development*, published in 1994. Buchanan's *Ten Shades of Green* now assumes its due didactic place within this legacy, largely because he demonstrates through well-chosen contemporary examples, most dating from the second half of the '90s, that there is no manifest reason why environmentally sustainable design should not be compatible with culturally stimulating and expressively vital results. Sustainability ought to be rightly regarded as a prime inspiration with which to enrich and deepen our emergent culture of architecture, rather than as some kind of restriction upon the fullness of its poetic potential.

Green Culture and the Evolution of Architecture

by Peter Buchanan

The most overwhelmingly urgent crisis facing mankind is the degradation of the natural environment, including the atmosphere and seas, and the concomitant problems of global warming and climate change. Virtually all other serious problems (such as over-population, hunger, social breakdown and inequality, the rise of diseases such as cancer and the spread of others, increasingly frequent and devastating 'natural' disasters such as storms and flooding) are part of this larger crisis, or closely related and subordinate to it. The continuation of what we would consider to be a comfortable and civilized form of human life depends on us, as individuals as well as collectively as mankind, changing our ways rapidly and radically so as to have a much more gentle impact upon planet Earth by cooperating rather than competing with its natural processes.

Contemporary buildings, like contemporary forms of urban development, are major contributors to the environmental crisis. Resolving this crisis will necessitate transforming all aspects of human settlement, including the construction of new buildings and the retrofitting of old ones, to be as green as possible. It is unthinkable that we can continue to plead that green buildings are unaffordable. Instead we must realize, and quickly, that we can no longer afford not to build green.

The green agenda will have immense appeal for architects, once they cease to resist it, because it regrounds architecture in real, immensely serious and urgent issues, and reconnects it with popular desires. These factors, along with the stimulus to fresh thought and creativity they bring, promise to reinvigorate architecture after an extended period of confusion, when many architects were lost pursuing the spurious dictates of fashion and theory. For everybody, green buildings also herald a much-enhanced quality of life, despite being devised to limit wasteful consumption. Together with being consistent with changes in human values, this is perhaps the most compelling reason for green buildings.

EVERY WEEK BRINGS FRESH EVIDENCE OF THE mounting severity of the global environmental crisis. It has already killed tens of thousands of people, and reduced millions more to misery as refugees from human-provoked 'natural' disasters. The problems confronting us form an all-too familiar and ever-expanding litany of impending disaster. Global warming is redistributing climatic systems and so annihilating ecosystems and their life forms, as well as bringing violent storms and summer brush fires, desertification, famine and the spread of killer tropical diseases, along with rising sea levels and the eventual inundation of many of the most densely populated parts of the globe and its greatest cities. Planet-wide pollution and toxic contamination of land, air and water are exterminating more species, and damaging immune systems and chromosomes leading to disease, deformities and infertility in humans and other creatures. Holes in the ozone layer cause cataracts and skin cancer, and threaten to blind insects, thus interrupting the pollination process on which all food cycles depend.

The list could go on and on. Of all the problems we face, these are only some of those to which buildings make an immense and direct contribution. But let us not extend or linger on this litany any further; the anger or debilitating sense of impotence that pondering it can provoke might distract from the main emphasis here, which is on positive and practical action through design.

Facing up to the scale and seriousness of these problems, it is clear that the central challenge of our times is to achieve sustainability. This quest will be a major factor setting the basic tone of the immediate future, and our success or failure in it will decide whether current generations will be admired or reviled in the more distant future. It is a challenge to all of us, individually and collectively: to our imaginations to conceive ways in which sustainability might be achieved, and to our political and corporate will to bring it about.

Yet what is really meant by sustainability? This is among the most abused of current buzzwords. There are architects and manufacturers whose designs and products achieve only small and narrow improvements in environmental performance, and yet are claimed to be sustainable. And there are politicians and corporations whose claims to be acting sustainably are based on the most nebulous, irrelevant and often cynical of reasons that achieve little beyond seductive advertising. Such all-too-common hypocrisies are very damaging, provoking complacency or skepticism, and so a tendency not to take seriously the quest for sustainability. Equally misleading and destructive is the charge that the quest for sustainability is essentially Luddite, and would involve a return to past ways of doing things. Certainly it would involve a new respect for and learning from the past, especially from ways of life once condemned as primitive and now seen as ecologically sound, socially stable and spiritually uplifting in their reverence for the earth and nature. Yet, in part because the planet must now support such a huge human population, sustainability can only be achieved by also moving forward, not just to a better quality of life in accord with emergent values, but often to using leading-edge technologies that are much more efficient than the 'dinosaur' industrial-era technologies that are still so prevalent in construction, manufacture and agriculture.

Basically, sustainability implies long-term viability. As the term sustainable is used today, sustainable developments, cultures, lifestyles or whatever, are those that do not over-tax the resources and regenerative capacities of the earth, thus leaving for future generations as much of nature's bounty and beauty as we now enjoy. Achieving such sustainability will require profound changes. For a start, industry, agriculture and city life could no longer depend on extracting and consuming resources, nor on releasing wastes (especially those that are toxic and/or destabilize natural conditions), at rates faster than they can be replenished, or neutralized and absorbed by nature and the earth. Instead we need to learn again to recognize and respect the earth's regenerative cycles and live only within their capacities. In fact, in the medium term at least, we need to allow for more than mere replenishment of what has just been harvested, and give nature a chance to repair the ravages wrought by our overly extractive and polluting economies and lifestyles.

Yet sustainability implies even more than this. Besides living within such natural limits, a sustainable society or culture (which might still be highly dynamic), cannot be vulnerable to excessive instability, social breakdown or a return to ways disrespectful of the earth – all of which would, by definition, render it unsustainable. Thus sustainability depends also on ensuring economic opportunity and social equity, as well as offering everyone a lifestyle that offers more than mere contentment, but also a sense of meaning and deep satisfaction. Instead of the inequalities and alienation of the present, people would be assured of the means to both fulfill their individual potential and gain a sense of connectedness, of intimate engagement with community and nature and so with their deeper psychological and spiritual selves. These economic, sociological, psychological, cultural and spiritual dimensions are all crucial to sustainability.

There can be no single, exclusive route to sustainability. Just as in nature biodiversity ensures the vitality and adaptability to cope with change and disruptive incidents, so sustainability cannot be achieved by the homogenizing and universalizing tendencies of the waning industrial era. Instead sustainability requires the continued vitality of the earth's various cultures and lifestyles which, although undergoing change and becoming ever more tightly interlinked and interdependent, should remain as diverse as the lands, climates and local traditions each arises from. What is crucial is both to learn from nature (thus conserving biodiversity and emulating it in the human realm) and to see the earth's needs and endless differentiations as primary, and humans as integral to these, arising from and supported by the earth as the conscious component of the flowering forth of evolution.

Mankind's socio-cultural evolution can no longer be driven blindly by the imperatives of the market, consumerism and technological development. Instead we must use the immense accumulated knowledge of our many sciences (including the human sciences such as psychology and anthropology, as well as all the physical and natural sciences) to be more self-consciously aware of and responsible for our own evolution, and so also that of the earth. Just as the great challenge of our times is to achieve sustainability, so that for all responsible and creative people is to participate in this process. Curtailing the profligate use of resources is being achieved by invention as much as by constraining diktat. Participating in this great adventure involves designing and inventing everything afresh: from new social rituals and institutions to such socio-cultural software as new management, economic, legal and tax systems; from new products and manufacturing processes to the transformation of most aspects of the built environment, including building components and transport systems. All of these are essential to, and will help bring about, the various sustainable cultures that will make up a sustainable global civilization. In turn, all of this involves redefining what it is to be human: no longer isolated and alienated from a subordinated and exploited nature, but ennobled and spiritually enhanced by the number and intimacy of our connections with nature. Such are the hugely onerous tasks, and immensely exciting challenges, the environmental crisis bequeaths to us all. These are potentially great gifts to artists and designers of all sorts—be they writers, painters, filmmakers, composers, choreographers, architects, urban or product designers, landscape architects or whatever—who might contribute in various ways to such cultural transformation, thus returning to these creative disciplines a dignity and purpose that has too often been missing of late. If we do manage to tackle the environmental crisis, then we are at the threshold of a creative renaissance. *Green Renaissance*

Clearly, architecture alone cannot bring about sustainability. Nor, for the same reasons that the quest for sustainability leads away from (and not towards) socio-cultural homogeneity, can there be a single, distinct green architecture or green aesthetic. (It is probably safer to talk about green buildings rather than green architecture or, perhaps worse still, sustainable architecture.) Nevertheless, because buildings inevitably impact upon and transform the environment, and because they both express and help shape the lifestyles and values of our culture, buildings and their architects have an immense role to play in the pursuit of sustainability. Yet many architects seem unaware of, or

reluctant to acknowledge, how much, and how unnecessarily, buildings contribute to the environmental crisis.

All architects know, of course, that new buildings consume vast amounts of land (all too often, prime arable land needed to feed growing populations), especially when part of the near-ubiquitous sprawl that also necessitates paving vast areas for roads and parking for the gas-guzzling, polluting automobiles it depends upon. Architects also understand that all this could be done far more wisely than now. They should also recognize that buildings consume and contaminate vast amounts of what is increasingly the most precious of resources, fresh water. They are also vaguely aware that buildings contain many materials that are toxic to manufacture or use (off-gassing noxious fumes—and even worse ones in the eventuality of fire—and polluting rainwater and soil) and that insulating materials and the refrigerants in air-conditioning units were prime culprits in destroying the ozone layer. But too few architects, particularly in the United States, seem at all aware that the construction and operation of buildings is responsible for nearly half the energy consumed by developed countries. Moreover, they seem untroubled by an awareness that this is largely unnecessary, as proved by the fact that elsewhere in the world it has become relatively commonplace for a building's energy consumption to be only a small fraction of that of its U.S. equivalent. Some European buildings even harvest the ambient energies of sun and wind so effectively as to be net energy exporters, sending the energy that is excess to their needs to nearby buildings or into the national electricity grid.

Contemporary architecture contributes to the environmental crisis in further, less direct ways than those listed above. Deep-plan air-conditioned buildings, hermetically sealed with tinted glass skins, suppress any sort of sensual contact between their occupants and the natural world outside. Such buildings also tend to be isolated from each other physically and aesthetically, and suppress any form of community life, both within them and in their surroundings. In alienating people from nature, each other and place, they alienate us also from such essential aspects of human nature as a sense of rootedness and connection. Thus these commonplace buildings, which are almost the contemporary American vernacular, not only mirror but also help entrench the mind-set that has perpetuated, or at least tolerated, the destruction of the natural world. Hence, the design of green buildings (once again, as with achieving sustainability in general) must involve more than resolving technical and ecological issues to also address social and spiritual ones.

Despite the urgency of the environmental crisis, and architecture's vast and varied contribution to both it and its eventual solution, most design professionals have been desperately slow to acknowledge, let alone take up, these challenges. There are several reasons for this resistance. In the last couple of decades the sort of architecture that has gained attention in the media and academy is that driven by form, fashion and theory (the latter itself largely the subject of fashion as theorists recycle the same limited set of ideas and sources) and has largely turned away from pressing realities, such as social and green issues. Indeed, the latter are stigmatized as untrendy, regressive and even reactionary. (Some academics have gone so far as to refer to eco-fascism.) A stereotyped notion of green buildings conjures up images of muesli-eating inhabitants with beards and sandals, and rudimentary forms of back-to-nature lifestyles—a caricature of the counterculture that pioneered much green experiment—as well as of crude and ugly buildings with which no urbane sophisticate or academic would wish to be associated. Although there is more than a grain of truth in such characterizations, they also show ignorance of developments in the rest of this world, such as those that are the focus of this book.

Fears that green design compromises the architect's creative prerogative, and charges that it is also essentially regressive, are commonly encountered. These reflect deep misunderstandings underlying much that is wrong with contemporary architecture. For too many today, creativity—supposedly expressed also in the architect's theories and formal predilections—is exercised as part of the architect's right to self-expression. However, another view of creativity has emerged, especially from the new sciences such as chaos and complexity theories. Creativity is not the prerogative of humans only; instead the whole unfolding of cosmological and natural evolution are seen as essentially creative processes, not just in the long term but moment by moment. Thus the truest and highest form of human creativity is to be found in participating in evolutionary process: transcending the ego in favor of the eco and playing a part in this constant flowering forth, and guiding it to the best advantage of the planet and all its creatures and peoples. Creativity of this sort is less the expression of individual genius than a participatory and collaborative process, a taking part in the larger unfolding of evolution and ecology—and in architecture this involves collaboration with engineers of various sorts, as well as with experts in the study of the natural world and, perhaps also, human nature and cultures. The resulting buildings are designed not as isolated objects but as a nexus of interactive processes with their surroundings. Designs emerge from studying the interactions with every aspect of their setting, from cultural context and local building traditions to climate, geology, hydrology, ecology etc. Such a design process often draws on up to the minute forms of scientific survey as well as leading- edge engineering which, in turn, depends upon state of the art computer modeling and predictive analysis. These studies feed rather than constrain creativity, grounding it in a myriad of novel factors to be resolved and synthesized, while the participative ethos ennobles rather than diminishes it. Rather than being regressive, such an approach is very much in tune with major changes in the

creativity

world view that science and the computer are affecting within our culture.

Nevertheless, green design has much to learn from the past, although there is nothing regressive about this either. Most major cultural epochs, such as that beginning with the Renaissance, are born in part from a rediscovery and reinterpretation of history. Just as the quest for sustainability is making us more receptive to the wisdom of other and earlier cultures, so green design can learn much from buildings of the past. Victorian buildings can be very sophisticated in their ventilation and heating systems, so it is little surprise that some recent green buildings in England (including some of those by Michael Hopkins) should rather resemble them. But, for the ways in which they are beautifully embedded in and adapted to their context and climates, it is usually vernacular buildings that are particularly instructive—both the vernacular of the local region and that of comparable biomes, those regions elsewhere on the earth with similar climate, vegetation and geology. Buildings of the past or other cultures are not to be copied slavishly, but rather studied so that their lessons and design devices might be reinterpreted to suit current construction technologies and lifestyles. The more recent past has much to teach us too, and not just in terms of negative examples. Many now forget that modern architecture grew in part from proto-green ideals, including the goal of creating community (most explicitly, and not always successfully, in the social housing built in Europe throughout the twentieth century) and of living in harmony with nature, whether this manifested in the physical form of the building or in the healthy open-air style of life it made possible.

Modern architecture always consisted of several streams, each of which had its own sources, which would flow independently, then join together to later branch apart again, thus creating a rich variety of intermingling approaches to design. If one proto-modern stream created an abstracted classicism, another advocated a return to Gothic architecture's direct expression of structure, construction and function. If one stream endorsed and celebrated industrial components and advanced technology, another lamented industry's despoliation of nature and its dehumanizing work conditions. John Ruskin, who has been called the father of ecology, was the key figure in the advocacy of the Gothic and the rejection of the negative aspects of industrialization that were already very visible in England. He saw the necessity of pursuing what we now call sustainability more than a century and a half ago. Thus in the "Lamp of Memory" (from *The Seven Lamps of Architecture*, 1849) he stated its moral imperative in terms that, except in language, are strikingly contemporary: "God has lent us this earth for our life; it is a great entail. It belongs as much to those who are to come after us, and whose names are already written in the book of creation, as to us; and we have no right by anything we do or neglect, to involve them in unnecessary penalties, or deprive them of benefits that it was in our power to bequeath."

Ruskin inspired the Neo-Gothic movement and the Arts and Crafts that followed it, and thus much of the ethos of what became modern architecture. (The young Charles-Eduoard Jeanneret, who was to become Le Corbusier, was profoundly influenced by Ruskin, as was Frank Lloyd Wright.) Ruskin's own architectural ideals were realized most directly in Deane & Woodward's Natural History Museum in Oxford (1855), in the creation of which he played a very active role, both as an advisor to the architects and as the patron who paid for much of the carved ornament. The museum is in an eclectic Gothic style, its main space an exhibition hall flooded with natural light through a roof of glass tiles supported by a Gothic-inspired structure of cast and wrought iron. The ornament of the structure and the carvings around the windows meticulously record local flora and fauna, and the colonnettes of the galleries overlooking the hall are each of a different British stone. The whole

Natural History Museum, Oxford (1855), Deane & Woodward

Entrance, Paris Metro (1899-1905), Hector Guimard

Taliesin East, Spring Green, WI (started 1911), Frank Lloyd Wright

building and its contents are both an education about and exaltation of nature. Once again much admired today, it was—along with Ruskin's writings—one of the original inspirations for two streams that have flowed through modern architecture.

The more vigorous and constant of these streams is what has come to be known as the biomechanical strand of modern architecture, whose origins include also the designs and writings of architects like Viollet-le-Duc. Rejecting the eclectic architecture of the preceding era, this initially sought more authentic expression in emulating the close fit between form, structure and function found in organisms, machines, or some formal fusion of these. After Neo-Gothic this stream flowed sinuously through Art Nouveau to eventually become the Vitalist strain of British High-Tech (with its exposed skeletal structures and knuckle-like joints, and shapely exoskeletal carapaces) and Renzo Piano's quest to bring an organicized technology into harmony with nature. Flowing more intermittently were the various tributaries of organic architecture, including that of Frank Lloyd Wright, which partly sprang from the Arts and Crafts and sometimes flowed close to the biomechanical and sometimes branched far away from it. Hence Wright's buildings were often built of local stone, nestled seamlessly into their sites and adapted to the local climate; yet they also made discriminating use of advanced construction and the technology of their times. Today, besides looking at vernacular architecture, with all its myriad passive devices of climate control, to learn about green design, modern architecture's biomechanic and organic streams (as well as others not discussed here) leave a rich legacy to reappraise and resurrect. It is hardly surprising that heirs to the biomechanical stream such as Foster and Partners, Michael Hopkins and Partners and the Renzo Piano Building Workshop are among the leading exponents of green design.

The reasons for the withering of modern architecture's green ideals are too various and too complex to be more than touched upon here. Most are not particular to modern architecture, but to modern culture generally. These include the whole restless ethos of capitalism with its constant drive to develop and redevelop, and the assumption underlying all industrial culture (capitalist, socialist or whatever) that growth is the ultimate good; the primacy of profit and the market, and the lack of value attached by economics to such 'natural capital' as clean air, fresh water and much else of nature's bounty upon which we are totally dependent; the tendency to short-termism in politics, planning and profit accounting; the tendency to reductive and instrumental thinking that tends to be so abstracted and narrowly focused as to miss the bigger picture; and the hubris brought by wealth, power and ever-improving technology that assumes that these can solve anything. In architecture, the critique of industrial society for its excessive exploitation of nature and humans, which had underpinned much early modernism, evaporated as modern architecture was co-opted, most willingly on its part, by commercial and governmental clients. These used the rhetoric of Functionalism to excuse the reduction of architecture to mere utilitarianism, minimal space standards and cheap construction. Buildings had value only in terms of efficiency of function (measured in profitable returns), and for as long as they functioned (remained profitable). Architecture shriveled into an autistic lack of concern with any larger issues. Compounding all these problems was the notion of an "international style"—that came with an equally destructive town planning accomplice, the Charter of Athens, promulgating mono-functional zoning— that virtually legitimized buildings quite unadapted to place and climate. Ironically, then, Functionalist buildings were often laughably inadequate in functional, climatic and constructional performance when compared with their nineteenth-century predecessors. [1]

With the introduction of modern industrial processes and products, many features of everyday building technology have become environmentally pernicious. These include the tendency to level plots and raze all vegetation and local features when constructing tract housing; the use of toxic, polluting and non-biodegradable materials as well as water-profligate plumbing fixtures, appliances and sewage systems; the voracious consumption of non-renewable resources; and, perhaps most especially, air-conditioning and the changes it has brought, especially the total dependency on electricity, the generation of which is a prime consumer of fossil fuels and source of carbon dioxide emissions. Air-conditioning brought about the second international style: the ubiquitous glass box, erected everywhere and at home nowhere. Its sealed and tinted glass walls sever contact with and awareness of sensual nature; and its deep plan removes people yet further from the outdoors to be totally dependent, at all times of day, not only on air-conditioning but also on energy-consuming artificial light. Worse still, the open or glass-partitioned interiors, devised for easy supervision, tend to squash many forms of social interaction. Architecture has been reduced to little more than energy-guzzling packaging; the façade, relieved of such essential functions as providing ventilation and shade, is a mere skin, its design merely a matter of current fashion; and the interiors are devoid of anything that might be called a room or processional sequence of spaces.[2] Little wonder that architecture collapsed into the arbitrary decorativeness of Post-Modernism.

For many people, the first intimations that energy-profligate buildings were not really viable in the long term came

---

1

Yet in many parts of the world, even the International Style was quickly adapted to suit to local conditions and climate and became an apt modern vernacular. Hence in tropical Brazil buildings arose on pilotis to better catch the breezes that wafted through their open, sun-shaded facades and the flowing spaces of their narrow, free-planned interiors.

2

This is not to say that air-conditioning will not remain a boon, and sometimes a necessity, especially in hot climates, polluted cities, art galleries and operating theaters. But careful design could ensure immense improvements in its energy-efficiency and eliminate the associated use of daytime artificial light, as well as ensuring that the air-conditioning be required only during extremes of heat and pollution. In fact, the tendency in some areas is to use mechanical ventilation only, rather than full air-conditioning, with chilled ceiling panels providing summer cooling.

with the Arab-Israeli wars of the seventies and the subsequent shortage, and price hikes, of oil. Initially this provoked a considerable response in the United States, resulting mainly in experimental low-energy houses—many self-built by counter-culture sympathizers, and usually inelegantly rough and ready in form and construction—along with some larger complexes, such as those commissioned by counter-culture hero Governor Jerry Brown of California. However, oil became cheap and abundant again, and (apart from a few notable exceptions such as the Intelsat headquarters in Washington by Australian architect John Andrews), architects working in the United States and their clients ignored the green agenda. Instead green design, as noted earlier, was stigmatized as a marginal counterculture pursuit, associated with the most inurbane and unrefined of construction. In more recent years a trickle of green designs have been built (and there have been important experiments in related areas such as in green systems of sewage treatment, such as those using constructed wetlands). Although some of the resultant buildings are thoroughly convincing in green terms, many are aesthetically graceless, so doing little to overturn many architects' prejudices against green design. Worse, this reinforces a vicious cycle whereby the better architects, who could create more formally accomplished buildings, remain wary of green design, so ensuring it retains its fringe status. Yet change is afoot and gathering momentum. With increasingly widespread and rapidly mounting interest in green design, and with mainstream architects and leaders in the profession beginning to show real interest, there is a gathering stream of promising projects on the drawing boards.

Nevertheless, the United States has fallen far behind other parts of the world, particularly Europe. There the development of green design has followed a very different course. The oil crisis of the seventies provoked some experiments in low-energy design, but not as many as in the United States. Since then, however, things have steadily escalated and more and more green buildings are being erected, mostly in northern Europe, though now in the Mediterranean countries as well. The architects now pioneering green buildings include some of Europe's foremost, such as Renzo Piano, Norman Foster and Michael Hopkins, as well as those beginning to win international acclaim such as Thomas Herzog and Françoise Jourda. Green buildings are far from a fringe pursuit, and are increasingly demanded by the most mainstream of clients. Indeed, for a building to have opening windows, fresh air, natural light and no air-conditioning conveys prestige. Such buildings include numerous flagship corporate headquarters, such as the skyscraper by Foster and Partners for Commerzbank in Frankfurt (p46), and the far from stereotypical glass box by Webler & Geissler for the Götz headquarters in Würzburg (p62), both in Germany. Even the most prestigious of governmental buildings are now green, such as Germany's reconstructed parliament, the Reichstag in Berlin (also by Foster and Partners), and Portcullis House, Michael Hopkins and Partner's building for members of Parliament, as well as one of the first of the current generation of green buildings, the European Investment Bank in Luxembourg by Denys Lasdun and Partners from the early 1980s.

This difference between the United States and Europe has been attributed to several things, all of which probably contribute to it. Fuel is more expensive in Europe, so the cost savings of energy efficiency are more pronounced. Utility companies and energy lobbies have not been able to suppress debate and information, and exercise as much power over policy, as they have in the United States. Some European countries have had strong clerical and office worker labor unions who demanded the physical work conditions their members prefer. A greater proportion of European businesses, both large corporations and smaller companies, build and occupy their own premises (rather than those of speculative developers) and so have direct interest in pleasant work conditions, diminished running costs and the benefits of a stable, happy and productive work force.[3] Much of Europe has a more temperate climate than large parts of the United States, and so it is easier to ensure comfortable conditions without resorting to air-conditioning. Europe consists of relatively small countries that demand action when pollution from a neighboring country defiles their rivers or kills their lakes and forests—in contrast to what can be resigned acceptance of home grown pollution. Leading European architects have generally been more concerned with social and technical issues, function and performance, than many of the most prominent American architects, whose concerns are more with form and theory. Engineers play a larger and more collaborative role in the design of buildings than in America, their proportionally larger fee affording them twice as much creative design time. In parts of Europe the banking system and funding of construction is somewhat less geared to the short term than in the United States, and so is less inhibiting of the long-term thinking and accounting essential to dealing with environmental issues. Generally too, European building, planning and tax codes are less likely to inhibit green buildings than some of those in the United States.

3

Whether this claim is correct or not, it is certainly true that the first significant green buildings were almost all for owner-occupiers - although now even some speculative buildings are designed to be green.

Also, in Europe in the last decade or so, green design has been given further impetus by the active encouragement of national and local governments (especially in Germany), and that of the European Union, which is firmly committed to working towards sustainability in general and energy efficiency in particular. Already in the seventies and eighties much of Europe introduced stringent energy-saving building codes, starting with such things as insulation standards. Then more recently the European Union, through its Joule 1 and Joule 2 programs, has paid for the research and experiment costs involved in developing and testing the designs of some high profile green buildings, reasoning that architecture generally would benefit from the widely publicized results. This is complemented by, among other initiatives, the Thermie program whereby the European Union contributes to the costs of experimental projects, in particular paying for the installation and testing of untried and still uneconomic environmental technologies. The rationale is twofold: that testing any technology promising considerable environmental benefit is an urgent imperative; and that some proven technologies would quickly become economic if demand was raised sufficiently to bring economies of scale, and further refinements, to their manufacture. The photovoltaic cells on both the Jubilee Campus of Nottingham University by Michael Hopkins and Partners (p74) and the Mont-Cenis Academy in Herne-Sodingen by Françoise Jourda Architects (p90) were paid for by Thermie grants. In the latter case, this helped make viable a nearby photovoltaic factory, with initial orders big enough to ensure its product will soon be sufficiently cheap to be economically viable (in terms of how quickly the cost of installing the photovoltaics is offset by the savings in utility bills).

Although Germany, Britain, the Netherlands and the Scandinavian countries are all independently committed in principle to achieving sustainability, and are each making considerable progress in reducing green house gas emissions, Europe still has a long way to go. By contrast, though, the United States resolutely refuses to address the issues. In 1997, under the Kyoto Protocol, the industrialized countries committed themselves to reducing greenhouse gas omissions by at least 5% below 1990 levels by 2008-2012. But, as the European countries recognize, this is far too little, far too late. (Scientists calculate that to avoid the worst consequences of global warming, cuts of 60-80% are required immediately.) Hence Germany's 1999 carbon dioxide emissions were already 15.3% below those of 1990 and it will easily exceed its own target of a 25% reduction by 2005. For all six gases covered by the Kyoto Protocol, Germany has already achieved an 18.5% reduction towards a goal of 21% by 2008-2012. Britain has cut its greenhouse gas omissions by 13%. It has now introduced new measures estimated to achieve a 21.5% reduction in carbon dioxide emissions by 2010. All this is being achieved relatively painlessly, mostly through the introduction of more efficient technology and careful design. By contrast, the carbon dioxide emissions of the United States (with less than 5% of the world's population and producing 25% of all carbon dioxide emissions) have increased by 21.8% since 1990. Instead of reducing its emissions in accord with the Kyoto Protocol, the United States proposes purchasing, and having considered as its own, portions of the reductions achieved by other countries. The United States also scuttled the ratification of the Kyoto Protocol in The Hague in November 2000 by insisting that the increased capacity to absorb carbon dioxide achieved through tree planting be considered as equivalent to a cut in emissions—despite the warning by many scientists that tree planting in temperate or cold climates is likely to increase global warming in the medium to long term. Even more recently, the new Bush Administration has announced that it has no interest in pursuing the Kyoto goals. The United States is thus abnegating totally its role as by far the most influential and emulated country in the world, and committing millions of people to a miserable future. It is foregoing the great benefits in improved quality of life that could have been achieved with little effort

beyond the exercise of the imagination.

The global environmental problems caused by the United States, however, result from far more than the irresponsible example it sets and its emissions of greenhouse gases and other pollutants. It also consumes far too much of the earth's resources generally, not just too much fossil fuels. If every person now living were to consume as much as the average United States citizen, it would require, by the most conservative estimates, at least another two of the planet Earth to support them. Americans, like everybody else, need to urgently reappraise their priorities and reconsider what they really want, now and most importantly, for the future. This should provoke a profound shift—away from the simple-minded consumerist pursuit of more, toward the far more discerning quest to obtain more of only what we really want – of what would make us truly and deeply happy.

It should be clear by now that green design, though not dauntingly difficult, cannot be achieved by any simplistic or formulaic approach: no single approach is likely to be adequate, let alone appropriate or even applicable, to all situations. Green design goes far beyond merely specifying efficient 'green' products, such as insulation, low-emissivity glass, water-conserving toilets, super-efficient mechanical equipment and non-polluting materials; and beyond also using replenishable, recycled and recyclable materials, recycling all rain and 'grey' water and planting on roofs. Green design both influences the basic design parti of a building, especially the cross-section and the elaboration of the outer envelope, and transcends mere energy efficiency and the minimization of pollution. Instead it must attend to a whole range of matters from the technical and ecological, to the economic and social, including even the cultural and spiritual.

This book spells out clearly both how broad is the span of these issues, and what they are exactly. Ten "shades," or aspects, of green are discussed in detail in the following

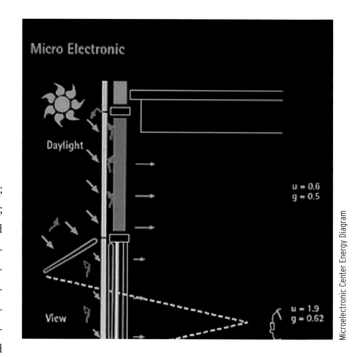

Microelectronic Center Energy Diagram

section of this book: 1–low energy/ high performance; 2–replenishable sources; 3–recycling; 4–embodied energy; 5–long life, loose fit; 6–total life cycle costing; 7–embedded in place; 8–access and urban context; 9–health and happiness; 10–community and connection. This list is intentionally somewhat hierarchic, starting as it does with narrowly technical issues, many of them quantifiable, and leading up through contextual and urban issues to largely qualitative socio-cultural ones. As listed, then, the issues could almost be seen as forming a conceptual ladder of steps of ever-broadening concern, with each step having to be considered in turn if pursuing a fully green approach to design. However, the position on the ladder does not indicate the relative importance of the concern. For example, as buildings become more energy efficient, embodied energy accounts for a proportionally larger part of the total energy invested in a building's total life cycle; yet embodied energy will probably remain less critical to the larger quests for green design and sustainability than the other issues listed directly before and after it in the sequence.

Two key issues are missing from the first set of ten shades: the roles of collaboration and of the computer. They are omitted both because they do not apply to all kinds of green design, and because rather than fitting into the hierarchy they relate to all steps of the ladder. With relatively traditional building types, such as houses and housing, satisfactory green design can be achieved by little more than updating vernacular building types and drawing on the accumulated empirical experience of the architect. But with larger and somewhat newer building types, for which there may be no vernacular precedent, devising a fully green design often requires a greater range of skills than any architect can provide. Engineers of various sorts make crucial contributions to the design, as might ecologists, hydrologists and geologists, horticulturists and landscape architects and various other specialists—including those with intimate knowledge of local climate, materials and crafts. To best synthe-

size their inputs, all these disciplines should contribute right from the beginning, some specialists (particularly the structural and mechanical engineers) participating by playing a fully creative role in a highly collaborative design process. This is relatively common practice in Europe. But learning to work in this way, with engineers as partners in the creative process, may be a challenge for U.S. architects.

The computer plays many roles in green design: during the design process it aids synthesis and prediction, and in the final building it constantly monitors and adjusts conditions. In early stages of design, the inputs of the various specialists might first take the form of surveys, whose findings might be weighted relative to each other and synthesized with the aid of the computer. Later, predictive modeling by computer and other forms of testing are also crucial. With conventional buildings, uncomfortable ambient conditions can be rectified by cranking up the air-conditioning. But because green buildings probably have no air-conditioning or other energy-guzzling equipment to fall back on, they have to be engineered with a precision made possible only by the computer. Ensuring that the building under design will remain comfortable, even after prolonged bouts of extreme temperatures, necessitates all kinds of predictive modeling and testing, studying fluctuations in temperatures, light conditions, humidity and so on. The completed buildings also depend heavily on computers. With the aid of myriads of sensors, the computerized 'building management system' monitors conditions inside and out; and with the aid of sophisticated software, that might use such things as 'fuzzy logic' and 'neural networks', it responds by constantly adjusting (with the aid of low-energy electric motors) the various mechanical devices that control the sun-shading, ventilation, flow of cool ground water in ceiling panels, and so on. In short, the computer makes it possible for buildings to be designed and to function as integral to—as a set of processes in reciprocal interaction with—its environment.

Increasingly, buildings under design are studied for their impacts on an area as much as a mile around them. The impacts on surrounding streets and buildings of, for instance, new wind patterns and pressures, or of exhausts such as steam and the condensation and increased temperatures these may cause, are modeled and analyzed. In part this is in acknowledgement that, because it is now possible to do this, others would be entitled to sue architects and clients for any disturbances caused by new buildings.

A third issue omitted from the first set of ten shades is the redefinition of comfort standards. This was omitted because it is probably only going to be an issue in the short term, before being widely accepted (as it already is in Europe). Consistent with industrial culture's obsession with standards and standardization, comfort used to be defined in terms of constant levels of temperature, humidity, air changes, light and so on. Yet research, no longer recent but previously little noted, about people's actual experience of comfort proved the common-sense notion that in winter, when more warmly dressed, people feel comfortable at lower temperatures than in summer, when more lightly dressed.[4] This might seem not only an obvious but also a rather trivial observation; yet complying with its implications alone can result in enormous energy savings, simply by lowering the levels of energy-hungry winter heating and

summer cooling. Other studies have shown that people prefer the sensual awareness of their bodies brought by gently fluctuating conditions (that open windows offer, for instance) to the homeostatic and anesthetizing constant conditions once considered to be ideal.

The buildings presented in this book and the exhibition it documents were selected to prove this diversity of potential solutions to the same green issues —and so also to show that resolving these is no straitjacket but rather a stimulus to creativity. This heterogeneity shows that there is no such thing as a green aesthetic, while the high architectural quality of the works shows that green buildings need not be synonymous with ugly and unrefined design. Some schemes, such as the Cotton Tree Pilot Housing by Clare Design (p56) and the four North American houses (by Lake/Flato, Rick Joy, Fernau & Hartman and Brian MacKay-Lyons p(102-111), are examples of the local vernacular reinterpreted for today; others, such as the Commerzbank tower and the Jubilee Campus, are the products of leading edge engineering and predictive computer modeling, by mechanical engineers Roger Preston and Partners and Ove Arup and Partners, respectively. Crucially, all the buildings illustrate well the enhanced quality of life promised by green design.

To facilitate instructive comparison, contrasting buildings of similar functional type were chosen. Thus there are two office buildings, both of them corporate headquarters in Germany that were purpose-built for owner-occupier clients. The tall tower of the Commerzbank headquarters is one of a cluster of towers in downtown Frankfurt; the Götz headquarters is a low-rise glass box—that at first glance seems only a refined version of what might be expected in its suburban, business park location. Yet despite these contrasts, the buildings have much in common. Both are naturally lit and ventilated through double-layered outer walls and internal gardens that bring the sensual presence of

4
Peter Buchanan, "Steps Up the Ladder to a Sustainable Architecture," *A+U*, no. 320, (May 1997), p. 6-13.

plants into the buildings while also serving as social foci. In the Götz headquarters this garden is in the central atrium whose glazed roof lifts and slides aside in summer; the Commerzbank tower's equivalent are the sky gardens that spiral around the central shaft that some people refer to as an atrium. Both buildings are cooled by chilled ceilings, and share a common spirit reflected in a very similar approach to details, as seen in particular in the glass balustrades. Both—with their bright and airy, naturally lit and ventilated, verdant interiors with ample provision for socializing—are green for more reasons than energy-efficiency; those very elements that are intrinsic to their energy efficiency (the sky gardens and central atrium) also enrich the buildings' social, sensual and spiritual dimensions.

The two housing schemes form another contrasting pair. Beyond concerns with energy efficiency and community, however, these have nothing in common. Because of their very different locations, this is as it should be: Slateford Green by Andrew Lee with Hackland + Dore is in Edinburgh, Scotland (p96), a city of cold northern European winters; the Cotton Tree Pilot housing, by the husband and wife team of Lindsay and Kerry Clare of Clare Design, is on the semi-suburban Sunshine Coast of tropical Queensland, with its year-round heat and humidity. Slateford Green is a single building, a looped wall of contiguous units wrapped around a single central court that, together with the conservatories overlooking it, is designed as a winter sun trap protected from the cold winds off an estuary of the Firth of Forth. Some of the Cotton Tree dwelling units also form a wall along the scheme's southern edge. But large gaps in the wall let the cooling breeze blow through it and between the units clustered on the rest of the site, as well as through the units themselves, while overhanging roofs shade windows and balconies. Here the cars are not kept to the perimeter, as at Slateford Green; instead motor courts penetrate the site. The motor courts, and the access routes from them to the dwelling units, form a dispersed communal realm quite unlike that of the singular central garden (ringed by private gardens) in Edinburgh. Yet thanks to careful design, both housing schemes promise a lively community life in an outdoor realm largely landscaped with indigenous plants (that tend to be better adapted and so 'greener' than imported ones).

Three institutes of higher learning are probably the most startlingly radical of the selected designs. Each looks very different from the other two, or indeed any other building. Each also exploits very different means to modulate its internal conditions and achieve energy savings. Almost disconcertingly strange, yet thrillingly so too, is the Minnaert Building by Neutelings Riedijk on the Uithof Campus of the University of Utrecht in the Netherlands (p84). Inside its rust-colored, sprayed concrete outer coat, wrinkled to express that it is only a skin, is a cavernous central hall. Half of this is occupied by a pool into which rainwater plunges, to then be circulated around the building to conduct away the heat given off by computers and occupants. The Akademie Mont-Cenis, a training center for local government employees in Herne-Sodingen in Germany, was built as part of the regeneration of the ex-rust belt of the Ruhr region. Standing in a new park over an abandoned coal mine, it resembles some cross between an enormous greenhouse and a contemporary temple, combining two design idioms that are usually polar opposites: crisply minimalist high-tech glazing and funkily rustic tree-trunk columns. Designed initially for a competition by Jourda & Perraudin in association with Ove Arup and Partners, and executed by Françoise Jourda in association with Hegger Hegger Schleiff, it offers inside a Mediterranean microclimate where students can enjoy a hedonistically semi-outdoor life in the elongated piazza between the residential and academic blocks. Another competition-winning design, the Jubilee Campus, by Michael Hopkins and Partners with engineers Ove Arup and Partners, is also built on what had been a derelict industrial site on which the architecture now sits in verdant landscaping. Here building, landscaping, ventilation system and the wind itself all work together as an inextricably interwoven whole to achieve a very complete and efficient green scheme that includes many devices that could be adapted and applied widely elsewhere. With its lakeside promenade and glass-roofed atria, this is a complex every bit as tailored around pleasant socializing as the Mont-Cenis academy.

Four North American houses together comprise one of the second set of ten shades. (A solitary house could hardly have represented the whole continent.) Each is in a different climatic region, and each updates or reinterprets the local vernacular to create houses that look at home in their settings and are well adapted to the climatic conditions. The Palmer House by Rick Joy, outside Tucson, uses the ther-

Regensburg House (1977-79), Herzog + Partner

Congress and exhibition center, Linz (1988-93), Herzog + Partner

Administration Building, Hanover (1996-99), Herzog + Partner

Hanover roof structure (1999-2000), Herzog + Partner

mal mass of thick adobe walls to absorb heat and stabilize the large diurnal temperature fluctuations of the Arizona desert. The South Texas Ranch House by Lake/Flato is in a somewhat less arid part of Texas and combines the patio format of local tradition with a freestanding pavilion that opens up to breezes off the adjacent river. The Westcott-Lahar house by Fernau Hartman is fragmented into elements that zigzag across an upper corner of the large site onto which the various rooms open. The back wall of the house is built of straw bales whose snug insulation is emphasized visually and psychologically by the resulting deep reveals to the small windows. These windows contrast with the large glass doors opposite that open onto the garden and terraces. The strong, simple form of the Howard House by Brian MacKay-Lyons commands its seaside site in West

Pennant, Nova Scotia, and adopts the matter of fact approach to available materials found in the local vernacular. All four houses remind us that it is only in relatively recent times that architects, and even then far from all of them, have chosen to ignore so disastrously climate and context.

Only two of the buildings presented are solitary examples of their functional types. These are Hall 26 by Thomas Herzog, an exhibition hall in a trade fair complex outside Hanover, Germany (p68), and the Beyeler Foundation Museum by the Renzo Piano Building Workshop, outside Basel, Switzerland. Yet they share some energy-saving strategies: both admit abundant natural light through their roofs; and both exploit the way air stratifies and rises slowly with increasing temperature, thus obtaining stable conditions in the lower portions of their interior volumes despite fluctuating conditions closer to the ceilings. Both buildings were selected to illustrate other points as well. The whole form of the exhibition hall, especially its longitudinal section, is an exact correlate of the efficient way it admits and reflects light as well as channels and exhausts the rising air. The museum exemplifies beautifully the ideal of a building embedded in its place so well as to seem to have grown from rather than been imposed upon its setting. Both buildings, which share an aesthetically satisfying crisp precision of detail, were also chosen because they are by architects who have designed other significant green buildings.

As well as for the reasons outlined above, the buildings were selected to show work from a range of architects: from established international figures to relative unknowns; and from those who have established a reputation for green design to those who are still relative novices in the field. All four of the established international figures—Norman Foster, Thomas Herzog, Michael Hopkins, and Renzo Piano are leaders also in green design. Just as instructive as comparing green buildings of similar functional type, is to study how each of these architects has explored and evolved different approaches to green design in successive buildings (an exercise recommended to all readers). Significantly, a number of the key green buildings by each of these architects, except for Hopkins, are in Germany, and the experience of building in that country had either led initially to or deepened each architect's embrace of the green agenda.

Thomas Herzog first embraced green design in the seventies, with some fine private houses. Since then his green buildings have included, as well as more houses, the Linz Design Center, an exhibition hall in Austria. For its roof he developed a special sandwich glazing that admits a high proportion of sunlight while excluding direct shafts of sun. Close to Hall 26, he has also built an energy-efficient office tower and a set of gigantic timber parasols under which

shelter smaller exhibition pavilions. The office building has a double skin of glazing, a now fairly common solution on German green buildings—and taken to an extreme of sophistication on the Götz Headquarters by Webler + Geissler. The parasols push timber construction to new limits and are supported by what had been three hundred year-old conifers. Felling huge old trees may not strike some as green, but Germany's foresters insist that it is, because such mature trees no longer absorb as much carbon dioxide as the growing trees that replace them.

Foster and Partners' first truly green buildings are in Duisburg on the Ruhr and, among other devices, again exploit double layers of glazed façade. After the Commerzbank came the reconstruction of the historic Reichstag in Berlin that once again houses the parliament of reunified Germany. Conspicuous outside is the new steel and glass dome that rises from the roof, as light and optimistic as the original dome seemed heavy and oppressive. Hanging down from the dome into the assembly chamber is the 'light reflector'. Its mirrored facets reflect natural light down into chamber while warm stale air is drawn up and out through its funnel-like form. As the dominant feature of the chamber, the light reflector hovering above the heart of Germany's government serves as a resonant symbol of its commitment to green ideals. As further green measures, the building powers its own electric generator with vegetable oils (releasing less carbon dioxide than captured by the plants providing the oil) and stores for recycling both warm and cold water in chambers insulated deep below the earth. Destined to be yet another of Foster's seminal green buildings is the Swiss Re office tower to be built in the City of London. This is an evolution of the Commerzbank designed for a corporation that has already commissioned and occupied green buildings in its native Switzerland. From this they know the advantages of green design lie in improved quality of life and social interaction, and so improved internal communications, as much as in dimin-

Microelectronic Center, Duisberg, Germany (1988-96), Foster & Partners

Reichstag, Berlin (1993-1999), Foster & Partners

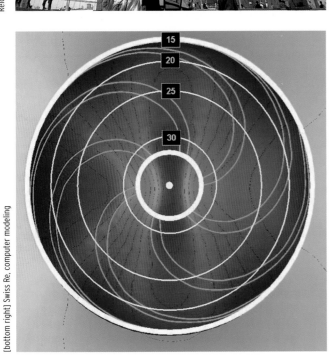

Reichstag, interior

[bottom right] Swiss Re, computer modeling

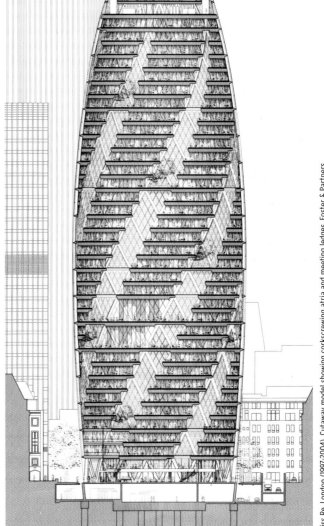

Swiss Re, London (1997-2004), Cutaway model showing corkscrewing atria and meeting ledges, Foster & Partners

ished running costs and environmental stress. Instead of a hollow shaft, Swiss Re will have a conventional core. But corkscrewing around its perimeter will be a series of naturally ventilated shafts with gardens on their stepping ledges. Meetings on these will be visible and inviting to those on the floors above and below them, so aiding the ease of communication that the clients value highly for the efficiency it brings. Like the Commerzbank, this is a design that has evolved in part by modeling its impacts upon an extensive area around it—in this instance by the mechanical engineers BDSP.[5] The rounded form of the building minimizes air turbulence and ground-level gusting, while the differing wind pressures around the circumference move air through the corkscrewing shafts without need for mechanical backup. In this case, the chillers were repositioned during design when computer modeling proved that they would sometimes have caused condensation on buildings some distance downwind.

Although it uses similar devices to those already explored at the Cité Internationale in Lyon, France, the Renzo Piano Building Workshop's first rigorously researched (with funding from the Joule 2 program) and designed green buildings are the office blocks of the large Potsdamer Platz scheme in Berlin. Shallow office floors, and an elongated glass-roofed atrium in the largest block, allow these buildings to be naturally lit and ventilated through opening windows. To break the force of the wind against these windows, and to intercept rain so that the windows may be safely left open at night to allow night time purging of summer heat, the taller facades are protected by an outer layer of adjustable horizontal glass louvers. In summer these can be opened to admit breezes, or be semi-closed to channel a stack-effect upward draft that draws cool air up the facades and into the open windows. In winter the louvers are closed to trap a layer of air, intermediate in temperature between inside

5
BDSP was formed by engineers who once worked for Roger Preston and Partners, who were mechanical engineers for the Commerzbank.

and out, against the building. This forms both an insulating layer and a source of warmed air for ventilation. All the offices include perimeter heating, and can have ceiling panels chilled by groundwater. These are used only in the extremes of winter and summer, respectively, when mechanical ventilation is available too. All rainwater is captured and used on planting, and grey water from handwash basins is used to flush toilets. The whole scheme is green in other ways too. It is a dense, mixed-use urban scheme (where people could live near to work, shops, etc.) that is also highly accessible by public transport – although these aspects are offset somewhat by the generous car parking provision and the large triple-level shopping mall dedicated to conspicuous consumption. The buildings are faced in terracotta that mellows with age and weathering and are flexible in plan, so exemplifying the ideal of long life, loose fit. Also, during construction most materials were brought to site by canal to minimize traffic congestion and pollution.

Another of Piano's seminal green buildings is the J M Tjibaou Cultural Center outside Nouméa, capital of the Pacific island nation of New Caledonia. It was built to conserve the artifacts and revivify the culture of the local Kanak people. Here enormous basket-like carapaces of curving, vertical timber ribs and horizontal wood slats cluster along a ridge between the open ocean and a sheltered lagoon and protect the center's main spaces. The prevailing winds off the sea sigh in the slats of these cases (as the architect calls them), which recall the spirit rather than exact forms of traditional Kanak huts (case in French). With the small scale and the optical vibration given by the slats and their varied spacing, these cases also establish a remarkable visual affinity with the surrounding vegetation that is venerated by the Kanaks. Thus the building is thoroughly embedded in place, in both its physical setting and in the culture it evokes in what is also a very contemporary design language. By adjusting banks of glass and wooden louvers behind the slats, these spaces are naturally venti-

Inland Revenue Center, Nottingham (1994), Michael Hopkins and Partners

Potsdamer Platz, Berlin (1992-2000), Renzo Piano Building Workshop

Tjibaou Cultural Center, Nouméa (1991-98), Renzo Piano Building Workshop

Portcullis House, London (2000), Michael Hopkins and Partners

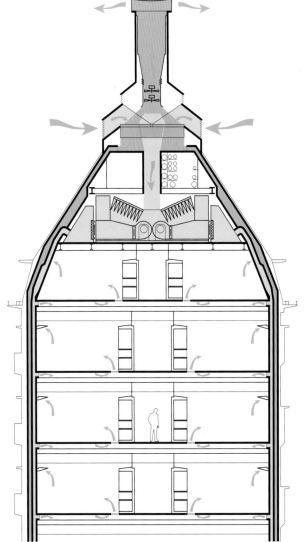

Portcullis House, section

lated no matter the strength and direction of wind—whether still days, when stack-effect ventilation is induced, or during typhoons from either ocean or lagoon. But for all their highly allusive poetry, these cases are also extravagant gestures; they stand as tall as the nave of a Gothic cathedral yet enclose smallish, single-story spaces. A Gothic cathedral, however, is also a single-story space; perhaps the best way to think of this building is as a temple to a new sensibility that has rediscovered a reverence for nature and for the traditional cultures that worshiped and lived in easy harmony with nature.

The Jubilee Campus was not the first milestone of green design by Michael Hopkins and Partners (another architect whose designs have benefited from research sponsored by the Joule 2 program). Another, also in Nottingham and also a commission won in competition, is the earlier Inland Revenue complex. To achieve long life loose fit, this is solidly built in brick and concrete and broken up into smaller blocks that can be leased independently if the original client no longer needs all of them. These blocks consist of a constant narrow section, allowing natural light and ventilation, folded around courts. Brick piers and light shelves both shade the windows from direct sunlight and reflect light deep into the offices; the brick piers and precast concrete ceilings also provide the thermal inertia to stabilize temperature fluctuations. Projecting from the corners of the blocks are cylindrical stair towers clad in glass blocks. As the sun warms these, the air inside rises by stack effect, its rate of flow—and so that of the air drawn through the offices to replace it—being adjusted automatically by the computer controlled raising and lowering of the stair tower's roof, below which the air is exhausted.

Portcullis House, opposite London's Houses of Parliament and providing offices for some of its members, was designed before but completed after the Jubilee Campus. Built of stone and precast concrete, this too has a high thermal inertia and is built around a court so that it can all be naturally lit. But because bounded by heavily trafficked, noisy and polluted streets, it does not have opening windows. Instead fresh air is drawn in above the roof ridge to be distributed down the façade and admitted through grilles in the raised floor. Stale air from under the ceilings is drawn up the façade to exhaust through heat exchangers in cylindrical chimneys that give the building a silhouette very similar to those of its neighbors.

Buildings such as those presented in this book and others by the same architects, as well as those by other architects exploring similar themes, are stepping stones to the future. They resonate with the epochal changes sweeping through our culture as evidenced in the emergence of the new sciences, the computer and how it is transforming our world and our understandings of it, and our deepest values. Yet this seems not to be fully recognized in the U.S., particularly in architectural schools and in the journals. This is because these tend to cling to a waning cultural paradigm or are seduced by what is merely a transitional one. The dying cultural paradigm is that of four hundred years of modernity, which emerged along with science and was consolidated during the Enlightenment. The single big idea underlying this paradigm, and defining its sense of reality, was that there is an objective reality, external to and unaffected by any observer. As this paradigm's weaknesses have become more evident and its fundamental flaws exposed (by, for instance, quantum mechanics) we have entered the age of post-modernity in which the cultural pendulum has swung to the opposite extreme and the emphasis is on subjective interpretation. In this cultural paradigm, in which everything is relative rather than objective, reality is a subjective projection or consensual hallucination. However, this paradigm is not the long-term successor to modernity; instead it is both its suppressed and contrary flip side and a hypermodern caricature of it. As caricature, it severely exaggerates some of modernity's greatest weaknesses, such as its propensity to excessive abstraction, and so alienation, arising in part from a lack of grounding in sensual experience. Underpinning the long term cultural paradigm emerging to replace modernity is a notion of reality that is both larger than and external to us, and yet is shaped in some degree by human participation. Reality in this paradigm is multi-layered and constituted by the unfolding and interlinked processes of cosmological, natural, socio-historic and personal evolution—a hierarchy whose lower levels we help create through our perceptions and actions, and whose higher levels we might eventually impact upon benevolently as we understand them and apply these understandings.

Most contemporary architecture conforms to the modern or post-modern paradigm. As modernity loses its credibility, many architects are fighting a rearguard action by reducing what was once a more encompassing and ambitious approach to architecture down to narrow certainties, such as with form and material (minimalism), technology (high-tech) or a degraded view of function (commercial viability). Others are post-modernists, not necessarily because they quote from history (classical or modernist) to suggest symbolic or semiotic resonances, but because their works are largely devised as interpretations and illustrations of some spurious theory rather than being grounded in a larger web of realities. The architecture of the emergent new long-term paradigm must be born from an evolutionary and ecological perspective, to be good for both planet and people and grounded in the complex and sensual realities of place and lived experience. Ultimately this is the most compelling reason that green buildings are the inevitable, inescapable future of architecture.

London, 2000

The Ten Shades

1 LOW ENERGY/HIGH PERFORMANCE

With increasing evidence of the escalating impact of global warming, the urgency of reducing emissions of 'green house' gases is now widely acknowledged. The single most effective way of achieving this is to ensure that buildings consume only a fraction of the fossil fuel-derived energy they use presently – which constitutes nearly half the total energy consumption of the developed world. Even better would be if buildings used no such energy at all, an ideal already achieved by some buildings. The familiar solution of high levels of insulation (with double and even triple glazing with low-emissivity glass, as well as insulation in roof and walls) saves much energy otherwise used for heating and cooling. But to make the further drastic savings now required, three other strategies need to be applied: the whole form and organization of buildings should be shaped to be far less dependent on fossil-fuel energy; any mechanical plant (if indeed there is any) should be as efficient as possible, as should be the whole system of which it is part; and the building and its environmental systems should harvest and be fuelled by constantly replenished ambient energies (replenishable sources).

Artificial lighting is a building's biggest consumer of energy, and then air-conditioning – which uses more energy in summer when used for cooling than when heating is required. Although high-efficiency light fittings cut electricity consumption considerably, it is impossible in conventional buildings to eliminate the need for night-time artificial lighting. But the use of day-time lighting can be reduced enormously, simply by abandoning the deep plan in multi-story buildings (perhaps by introducing atria or open courts), as well as by installing sensors that prevent lights being used unnecessarily. To let in lots of light, windows should be big; they then need to be shaded by overhangs, or by being recessed, so that high summer sun is excluded but low winter sun is admitted. Today, projecting horizontal sun shades often double as light shelves bouncing light from their upper surface onto the ceiling inside and so deep into the room, thus lessening the need for daytime artificial light. (With or without the help of light shelves, higher ceilings also let light deep into a room, as well as bringing other energy saving advantages.) Brise-soleil are making a comeback. Properly designed, they are both sun shades and light shelves, providing ideal conditions of shading and sun penetration, eliminating the need for tinted glass while reflecting glare-free light deep into the building. They also guide air through them and the windows behind, as well as up the façade to cool it in summer, and yet break the force of the wind and intercept rain so that windows can be left open day and night.

Forsaking the deep plan also allows air-conditioning to be dispensed with in favor of natural ventilation, with the added advantage that this can be under the personal control of each building occupant. This natural ventilation can be assisted by passive (non-mechanical) or active (mechanical) systems. For greatest efficiency, both would be displacement systems, exploiting the natural tendency for air to stratify in layers of different temperature. Combined with high ceilings (as at the Beyeler Foundation Museum, Jubilee Campus of Nottingham University or Mont-Cenis Training Center), this might allow temperatures to vary considerably in a room's upper volume from where the air is extracted, while always remaining equable in the lower, inhabited parts where the fresh air is admitted. Passive systems might include deliberately induced internal stack effects (upward currents of warm air rising through tall volumes), or exploit the wind outside to create negative pressure due to the Venturi effect. Independently or in unison (as at both Hall 26 and Jubilee Campus), such effects can help suck air through and out of a building. Mechanical systems might aid (as in the last two examples) or be unaided by such effects. Yet even in the latter case they could prove more energy efficient than purely passive systems; this is because the power used to drive them is more than offset by the energy from lights, computers, people and sunlight recaptured by the use of heat recovery systems.

People have been found to accept, even enjoy, more

widely fluctuating temperatures in naturally ventilated buildings, particularly when these conditions are under personal control, than they will accept in air-conditioned ones. Recognizing this factor alone results in enormous energy savings. Even greater savings result from recognizing that people do not prefer buildings, whether naturally or artificially ventilated, to be kept at a constant, supposedly ideal, temperature. Instead, extensive testing has confirmed the common-sense notion that people prefer buildings to be somewhat cooler than this ideal in winter, when they are warmly dressed, and warmer in summer when they are more lightly clad. Nevertheless, naturally ventilated buildings have to be designed to always remain within the range of comfort, and so may need occasional heating and cooling. However, in temperate climates the need for this can be immensely reduced, and sometimes eliminated entirely, by exploiting the thermal inertia of heavy structures. These can absorb immense amounts of heat while warming up only slowly, and then dissipate heat while cooling down equally slowly.

Exposing such a structure internally (by not including suspended ceilings, for instance – as at the Jubilee Campus, or the inner buildings of the Mont-Cenis Training Center) allows it to absorb heat from a room so that on warm days no further cooling is required. The structure can be cooled by letting night air into the room, or cavities in the structure, so that it is ready to absorb more heat the following day. (Monitoring of a number of recent buildings confirms this system as very effective.) In winter the structure may radiate heat if the temperature in the room falls quickly. Basically, the thermal inertia of the structure smoothes temperature fluctuations and avoids extremes. There are also buildings that now use the thermal inertia of the earth below them to achieve such effects, or use underground rock stores or pools of water as thermal reservoirs. In tropical climates an antithetical strategy is required, and the thermal inertia of a building is minimized so that it retains as little heat as possible and cools down quickly in the

evenings. Here, rather than expose a heavy structure to heat, the weight of the structure is minimized and it is shaded from the sun. The result is buildings with layered roofs and walls (as at the Cotton Tree housing), the outer layer being merely a sun screen shading the load-bearing and weather-excluding elements.

No matter how effective all these strategies, there are climates and locations in which some heating and/or cooling is required. However, careful design will considerably reduce both the period these are required and the energy they consume, which in any case can be drawn from ambient energies. Thus heating can be achieved by water heated by solar panels, which might (if winter conditions necessitate it) have been stored since summer underground. In summer, cooling can be achieved by using heat from a similar source to drive refrigeration units (as at the Götz Headquarters), and/or by the increasingly common solution of pumping cool water (often ground water) through ceiling panels (as at the Commerzbank, Götz Headquarters and Minnaert buildings), or by various forms of evaporative cooling (as at the Jubilee Campus).

REPLENISHABLE SOURCES
Much of the destruction wrought on the planet by industrial civilization is because it has used unreplenishable sources for energy (fossil fuels in particular) and building materials (such as hard woods felled faster they can be regrown – if they are replaced at all). To live more gently on the earth we need to use the non-depletable ambient energies of the sun, wind, waves and gravity (as in hydro-electricity), and use constantly replenished materials such as woods from sustainably managed sources (as at the Jubilee Campus and Mont-Cenis Training Center), or near inexhaustible materials such as mud, clay (for bricks) and sand (for glass). Green architecture is designed to use such sources.

Much of the energy consumed by buildings might soon be generated from un-depletable sources, with electricity from wind farms, hydro-electric, geo-thermal or biomass (vegetal waste) burning plant and wave or tide driven generators. Yet it could be that less of such power is needed, because the buildings themselves will harness the ambient energies around them. After all, a building only uses a tiny percentage of the energy that impacts upon it in the form of sunlight and wind. It is commonplace for buildings to be warmed by winter sun, admitted directly or via a conservatory, and by water heated by solar panels. Heat from the latter source is also used for cooling and refrigeration plant (as at the Götz Headquarters). Already some buildings generate electricity by photovoltaic cells (as at the Jubilee Campus and Mont-Cenis Training Center) or by harnessing the wind outside, and others are already under design that will use internal stack-effect convection currents for the same purpose. Buildings already stand that generate more energy than they use, exporting the excess to neighbors or the national grid (as do the last two examples cited). Already with today's technologies, it is feasible for buildings in much of the world (and most of the U.S.) to be self-sufficient in energy terms, or even energy exporters.

However, it would be very difficult for most buildings to made totally of replenishable materials. Yet a far greater proportion of each building could be made from such materials, as well as those that have been recycled and/or lend themselves to recycling.

Materials from replenishable or near inexhaustible sources, such as wood or clay, often improve with age and so encourage such recycling.

3 RECYCLING: ELIMINATING WASTE AND POLLUTION

In nature there is no waste. In the organic cycle, the 'waste' from one creature or process is the nutriment for the next. Today, we not only consume or destroy nature's resources faster than they can be regenerated, but we give nothing back to nature. Instead we further burden it with waste and toxic pollution. We have to stop this or urgently learn how waste and pollution can become resources to be recycled.

Obsolete buildings, their materials and components tend to be treated as waste. Yet many of the materials could be recycled, and new buildings and the components they are made from be designed (according to long life, loose fit precepts) to be robust and adaptable enough for a long life. These buildings would also be designed so that if they were to be demolished, their materials and components could be readily recycled – as is already the case with some European automobiles and kitchen appliances. Indeed, some Scandinavian manufacturers of building components already buy back and recycle or dispose of any of their products, no matter the age or condition.

Many modern building materials and components are not only non-recyclable, they are toxically polluting in manufacture and when installed, poisoning the environment and their occupants (hence 'sick building syndrome'). Any green architecture would foreswear materials that are polluting to the air, earth or water, or to people, plants and other creatures. They and the materials they are made of would also be devised to be cleaned with non-polluting materials, unlike so many of the cleaning materials now in common use. Though the earth is mostly covered with water, less than one percent of this is fresh and most of this is now seriously polluted. Yet buildings continue to use and pollute vast amounts of water. Green buildings conserve and recycle water in a variety of ways. Rain water is captured and used for plants and flushing toilets; 'grey water' from showers, baths and basins is also used to flush toilets or repurified through reedbeds that are part of the buildings' landscaping.

Already in some countries a major planning and urban design concern is to locate buildings and industrial plant so that the waste from one is a resource for the next. At its simplest level, the heat from power stations, garbage incinerators or industrial plant is used to heat neighboring buildings. There is now a whole town in Denmark where the waste from one factory or plant is used by the next, thus eliminating waste and pollution and creating the constant recycling of nature that we must learn to emulate.

4 EMBODIED ENERGY

Buildings not only use energy, it also takes energy to make them. This energy is embodied energy, which is all the energy required to extract, manufacture and transport a building's materials as well as those required to assemble and 'finish' it. As buildings become increasingly energy efficient, the energy required to create them becomes proportionately more significant in relation to that required to run them. This is particularly true because some modern materials, such as aluminum, consume vast amounts of energy in their manufacture.

The building material with least embodied energy is wood, with about 640 kilowatt-hours per ton (most of it consumed by the industrial drying process, and some in the manufacture of and impregnation with preservatives). Hence the greenest building material is wood from sustainably managed forests. Brick is the material with the next lowest amount of embodied energy, 4 times (X) that of wood, then concrete (5X), plastic (6X), glass (14X), steel (24X) and aluminum (126X). A building with a high proportion of aluminum components can hardly be green when considered from the perspective of total life cycle costing, no matter how energy-efficient it might be.

From the perspective of embodied energy, every building, no matter what its condition, has a large amount of energy locked into it. This is yet another factor in favor of conserving and restoring old buildings, and for designing long life, loose fit buildings that easily accommodate change. Also, because the energy used in transporting its materials becomes part a building's embodied energy, this is an incentive to use local materials thus helping the building to be embedded in place.

5 LONG LIFE, LOOSE FIT

As well as conserving nature and energy, green design is concerned with conserving old buildings, and with new buildings that lend themselves to being conserved. There are several reasons for this, including conserving the embodied energy in the building fabric and increasing the financial returns on the initial investment. It also prevents unnecessary disruption of the neighborhood, allowing buildings to settle into place, patinate and mellow with time, become embedded in vegetation and accumulate associations in the memories of those who come in contact with them. Also, designing such buildings forces architects to think long term about the legacy to future generations, and to transcend the utilitarian and the fashionable to consider how to make buildings that will always be cherished, that people will identify with and always wish to reuse and conserve.

It is in large part because historic buildings were conceived in such terms that they are so treasured today. Most historic buildings are proving more adaptable to reuse than buildings from the recent past. This is because the older buildings were not built to minimal space standards and ceiling heights; and they avoided the debilitating extremes of either being tightly tailored to function and the mechanical equipment that serviced them, or of being quite without character so as to be totally flexible. In today's parlance, they are long life, loose fit (and the latter is not the same as no fit). They were also built with materials that lasted and even improved visually and in tactility with age.

Green buildings should thus also be long life, loose fit: generously accommodating and generic in organization so as to adapt to, yet set a dignifying framework for, change over the generations; hospitable and socially convivial rather than merely utilitarian; pleasant in character and relatively timeless rather than saddled with gratuitous gestures that quickly become passé. And they would be largely made with robust materials that mellowed with age and weathering, as generally do those with low embodied energy and from replenishable sources, or those that are virtually inexhaustible. A good example of such architecture is the Jubilee Campus.

6 TOTAL LIFE CYCLE COSTING

Green thinking takes the long-term view and looks at the

larger impacts of any action, such as constructing a building, on the environment and society. Total life cycle costing is an essential part of such holistic thinking which is intrinsic to green design.

Today, the discipline of total life cycle costing is still not often applied in this broad, holistic sense, but in a narrowly economic manner. Yet merely this is an asset for showing that even in the strictest financial terms green design is a sound investment. It proves that a building's initial capital cost amounts to only a small fraction of the total cost of running and maintaining it. Over the years, the savings in utility bills achieved by energy efficiency can prove equal to or exceed what the building originally cost. Also, buildings that require less maintenance, and/or are easier to clean, can recoup several times over any extra investment necessary to achieve this. If the wages, contentment and performance of the building's occupants are considered, the cost benefits of green design can prove staggering. During the life of an office building, factory or hospital, the salaries of those who work there amount to several times the building's original cost. Hence, the diminished absenteeism and staff turnover, along with the increased productivity, typically reported of green buildings are compelling economic (as well as social and political) reasons for investing in green buildings. Thus a building like the Commerzbank, which was not cheap to build as office towers go, will probably prove a shrewd and profitable economic investment, which has brought the client much prestige.

Increasingly, total life cycle costing is considered in terms that are broader than economic, and longer term than merely that of the building's life. Instead it is concerned with assessing the total costs – including those to society, local community and individuals, ecology and larger environment, the psyche and sense of the aesthetic – of every aspect of the building, right from the extraction, manufacture and transport of its materials, through its erection and useful life to the ultimate recycling of its materials or their degradation back to earth. To Americans such thinking

might sound like pie-in-the-sky. But it has already been adopted, at least as an ideal, by some Scandinavian governments and corporations, as well as the best European architects; and it will most likely rapidly become a legal obligation in much of the developed world. Only by applying such a discipline can we be sure of leaving a world fit to sustain and be enjoyed by future generations.

7 EMBEDDED IN PLACE

A green building cannot be designed in the abstract and imposed on a place. Instead of being conceived of as a self-contained object, design focuses on elaborating a dense web of complex symbiotic relationships with all aspects of the building's setting. The inspirational ideal is to imagine a building that seems to have grown in place in intimate interaction with its surroundings, and often also with deep roots in the accumulated wisdom of the local culture and its vernacular buildings.

This implies no single, ideal design approach but a spectrum of them. These range from that informed by knowledge of the place, its local materials and building traditions, and drawing on the personal experience of the designer, to an approach based on rigorous surveys of all aspects of the site and then predictive analysis that draws on state of the art computer modelling. Informing this whole spectrum of approaches is the intention to create an architecture that has no homogenizing effects, but helps every part of the earth to be yet more richly differentiated, yet more resonant with the particularities of a unique place. And though the two extremes characterized above are very different – one drawing on tradition, rule of thumb and intuition, the other on leading edge science and engineering - both are equally relevant when applied appropriately. The former approach is best suited to small scale and familiar building types, such as houses, and might consist merely of continuing or updating the vernacular. It is best applied by architects who already know their locale intimately and usually consists of adapting and improving traditional devices for tempering the climate and using local materials. The Cotton Tree housing and four American houses exemplify this approach, which reinterprets tradition through a contemporary sensibility and so as to suit contemporary lifestyles.

The latter design approach, the opposite extreme of the spectrum, is best suited to large scale and/or less traditional building types and draws on the latest scientific understandings and survey techniques as well as the computer's capacity for synthesis and predictive modelling. It proceeds by extensive study of the site and surrounding area, surveying what is both above and below the ground (the microclimate and ecology, geology and hydrology, and so on) and then assessing (through predictive modelling using sophisticated computer programs, wind tunnel testing of models, etc.) how to minimize any negative impacts on these. The building is thus designed to fit into and be an intrinsic part of the locale, the architect attending to all the many interactions with the setting, microclimate, topography, vegetation and local traditions as much as with the building's functions and abstract formal properties. Design almost recapitulates the process of an organism evolving to fit an econiche in a way that benefits all of its species, the building being inserted as gently as possible to establish the complex reciprocities of a true symbiosis between itself and every aspect of its setting.

(This of course is an ideal that is difficult to achieve fully. The Jubilee Campus is a product of such predictive modelling and reciprocities with ambient forces, but here the natural setting is one that was also created artificially. The Beyeler Foundation Museum, also in an artificial nature, is another building beautifully embedded in its context.)

Such extraordinary sensitivity to nature and emulation of its processes is made possible by leading edge technology. (The key quest for such technology is shifting from conquering nature to refining our understanding of it and capacity to act in harmony with it and its regenerative processes.) Today, when designing a skyscraper (such as the Commerzbank), its impact in terms of wind disturbance, raised temperatures or condensation can be, and increasingly is, studied on buildings and outdoor spaces a mile or more away. The impetus to do this is partly legal: the fact that such modelling is now possible means that designers (architects and engineers) and their clients who neglect to take such care can be sued for any distant disturbances caused. Once it is recognized that nature also should have its rights, its health and interests protected, and these become enshrined in law, we will learn yet more about how to seamlessly embed buildings in their place with minimal negative impact.

8 ACCESS AND URBAN CONTEXT

Transport, particularly automobile use, is the second biggest consumer of energy, after buildings. Even the most energy-efficient work place, if sited miles beyond access by public transport, would do nothing to ameliorate pollution and global warming – at least until low-energy or non-fossil fuel burning automobiles become a reality. Such a building would contribute even less to diminished production of greenhouse gases if it were removed from local shops, restaurants and opportunities to socialize, and housed none of these itself. A building's location in terms of its accessibility and proximity to a range of other functions is thus critical in determining how green that building can be.

In the larger quest for sustainability, the design of our cities and other forms of settlement, the relationship of these to each other and to their regions, are as crucial as is the design of individual buildings. But, no matter how important such concerns of city, regional and even national planning and the issues they raise in relation to individual buildings, these are too many and too complex to be more than briefly touched upon here, especially as the implications often seem contradictory unless explored in considerable depth. For instance, many argue that sustainability suggests civic compactness and high densities. These consume less land, make efficient public transport and walking possible, and allow the rich mix of local uses, including shops and cafes, which is now an essential part of a vibrant community life. According to this logic, 'brownfield' sites should all be rebuilt and suburban areas increased in density. Yet the counter arguments are just as compelling, and a good case can be made for using brownfield sites and selective demolition to establish swathes of wild landscaping cutting through the city. These would bring many benefits, allowing city dwellers to retain some contact with nature, providing pleasant alternative routes by which to walk or cycle through the city, allowing wild life to flourish and for it too to move through the city, tempering the city's microclimate and absorbing noise and carbon dioxide. However, these contrasting strategies are not mutually exclusive and if treated as essentially complementary could combine in creating a new kind of city that is both more convivial for humans and more supportive of nature.

Too many architects extrapolate from the fact that half the world's population now live in cities the dubious conclusion that the inevitable future is of an ever-greater proportion of mankind living in ever-bigger cities, many of them the exploding megalopoli of the developing world. But, not only do such cities have, in the short term at least, huge social problems, the planet cannot support them. The reason is simple. Each such city has a huge 'ecological footprint', defined as the area necessary to feed it, supply the materials for its buildings and industry, absorb its wastes and convert its carbon dioxide back into oxygen. The discipline of measuring these ecological footprints shows them to be so vast that collectively they are over-taxing the earth's resources and regenerative capacities.

One of the most urgent challenges for architects, planners and politicians is to reduce the ecological footprints of cities and seek a variety of other forms of human settlement, or networks of settlements. These should be less taxing in their impacts on the earth, yet also exploit our increasingly miniaturized and etherealized technologies so that everybody everywhere will enjoy all the benefits of contemporary life. Just as green buildings are conceived of as intimately related to their settings, so such settlements,

like the cities of the future, will be considered along with their hinterlands as an indivisible organic whole. What will matter is the long term viability of both settlement and hinterland, and the health and happiness of their human and non-human inhabitants.

9 HEALTH AND HAPPINESS

Too many contemporary buildings, particularly work places where people spend the greatest part of their lives, are not only bad for the environment around them, they are bad for the people inside them too. Their occupants are often not only deprived of the joys of fresh air and natural light, and do not have personal control over the artificial substitutes for them, but they are without even a view to the outside. Designed only for efficiency, as defined in the most squalidly narrow terms, such buildings do nothing to foster any sort of community life within them. They do nothing to ground or expand people in a sense of contact with the surroundings and nature, with each other or even with the building itself. But such buildings are not only profoundly alienating and joyless, and so psychologically unhealthy, they are bad for people's physical health too. Besides including in their construction many materials that are toxic, or are toxic to manufacture, the interiors of such buildings off-gas noxious fumes and deprive people of the essential health benefits of the full-spectrum of natural light. These, and other still-controversial effects, contribute to what is commonly known as 'sick building syndrome', itself still the subject of some controversy.

By contrast, green buildings are not only good for the planet and cheap to run, they are also good for people – which makes them yet more economical. Companies and corporations moving into green buildings typically report a considerable drop in absenteeism (in a number of monitored cases, about 15 percent), often as much because workers are (for obvious reasons) healthier as well as being happier. They also report reduced staff turnover, thus saving money on constant retraining, and improved productivity. This latter is often the most dramatic and profitable of these benefits, but also the most difficult to accurately quantify.

The reasons for these benefits are several. At the most basic level, people are healthier because they do not work in an environment full of toxic materials and fumes. The psychological and social dimensions are important too. People cherish a sense of contact with the outdoors and its ever-changing conditions, as recognized in the 'blue-green' laws coming into force in various parts of Europe, whereby all workers are entitled to a view of the sky and vegetation. People prefer it yet more if contact with outdoors extends to opening windows, as well as the control over personal comfort conditions these bring. (The concomitant recognition of people's enjoyment of fluctuations in temperature not only brings energy and cost savings, but has led to a long-overdue redefinition of comfort standards. These are now not understood in terms of constant ideal conditions (which deaden the senses), but of the pleasures of gently varying sensual stimuli.)

The best green buildings might go much further, perhaps by bringing nature indoors in the form of planting, and including a range of social foci that that foster a vibrant communal life. The Commerzbank and Jubilee Campus each use a single repeated element to achieve both these goals. The sky gardens of the former bring in not just natural light and fresh air, but also the close proximity of plants to even offices high up in the tower, while also serving as social foci; in the latter complex, the atria serve similar multiple functions, adding the communal dimension that is intrinsic to a fully green architecture and the happiness and good health (mental as well as physical) it promises.

The creation of a green architecture, then, is much more than a merely technical issue: it is essentially concerned with delivering a much-enhanced quality of life, to be enjoyed now and capable of continuing into the future. It is only this broader vision of cultural transformation promised by a truly green architecture that will convince people to move forward to sustainable lifestyles.

10 COMMUNITY AND CONNECTION

The mind set that tolerated our destruction of the natural world and the legacies left to us by history depended on the suppression of a sense of connection with each other, nature and the cosmos, as well as to past and future generations. If a green architecture is to help bring about a sustainable culture, it must regenerate a sense of community and connection to, even communion with, the natural world.

The opportunity for communities to form and function needs to be designed into all levels of the built environment, and is a challenge to planners and urban designers as well as architects. At the architectural level, all sorts of building types increasingly stress the community dimension. In part this is because as we do more and more at home – including work, play and exercise – the major reason to go elsewhere is to meet other people. Hence green buildings like the Commerzbank and Jubilee Campus give great emphasis to very pleasant communal facilities that will help generate that sense of community. And housing schemes like Slateford Green and the Cotton Tree housing are more than a collection of dwelling units, but are shaped to generate a varied and active community life.

In all these schemes, the same elements that shape community life also give a sense of connection to nature. A major element of green architecture should be not just to work with and be gentle to nature, but also to make conspicuously visible its workings and cycles. This will educate people about and make them more sensitive to nature, and also give them a sense of connection with and rootedness in nature. The ultimate ideal would be an architecture that fostered in various ways a deep sense of communion with nature and the cosmos. Such an architecture is not only good for the planet, it is also the only one in which people can flower into their full potential, discovering themselves in interaction with others and opening into contact with the most ennobling of human sensibilities as they experience their connections with the larger scheme of things, and the ways in which this unfolds from past into the future.

1 LOW ENERGY/HIGH PERFORMANCE

Achieved by making maximum use of natural light and ventilation as well as by using sunshades and/or light shelves, insulation and multi-layered façades and roofs, appropriate thermal inertia (high in temperate climates, low in tropical), solar heating, evaporative cooling, water chilled ceilings, displacement ventilation in tall volumes and the redefinition of comfort standards.

2 REPLENISHABLE SOURCES

Buildings as well as power plants can harvest the non-depletable ambient energies of the sun, wind, waves, gravity and geo-thermal power. Build with constantly replenished materials, such as wood, or near inexhaustible ones, such as clay (for brick) and sand (for glass).

3 RECYCLING: ELIMINATING WASTE AND POLLUTION

Reuse old building materials, design buildings that are easily reused and build them with easily reused materials and components. Recycle water and heat. Avoid materials that are toxic in use or manufacture, or need to be cleaned with toxic materials.

4 EMBODIED ENERGY

With energy efficiency, embodied energy becomes increasingly significant in relation to life-time energy use. The material with lowest embodied energy is wood, then brick, and that with most embodied energy is aluminum.

5 LONG LIFE, LOOSE FIT

Built with materials that endure and improve with age, green buildings not only accommodate change easily but are relatively timeless and pleasant in character so that people prefer to conserve them.

6 TOTAL LIFE CYCLE COSTING

Accounts for more than initial capital costs, to include running and wage costs. Also looks at costs to environment and society of all aspects of the building, right from extracting the materials to their eventual degradation back to earth.

7 EMBEDDED IN PLACE

Green buildings fit seamlessly into, help reintegrate and minimize negative impacts upon their settings. Depending on the projects, drawing on local wisdom and updating the vernacular, or using scientific surveys and predictive computer modelling, are equally appropriate approaches to achieving this.

8 ACCESS AND URBAN CONTEXT

To be green, a building must be close to public transport and other quotidian uses. Achieving a green built environment will involve rethinking not just buildings, but cities and other forms of human settlement.

9 HEALTH AND HAPPINESS

Natural light, fresh air and absence of toxic materials and off-gassing combined with the contact with outdoors and community life makes occupants of green buildings healthy and happy. This leads to diminished absenteeism and staff turnover as well as increased productivity.

10 COMMUNITY AND CONNECTION

To help achieve a sustainable culture, green buildings must regenerate a sense of community and connection with the natural world thus giving a sense of belonging and chance to discover one's deeper self in opening up to others and the cosmos.

Climate: High Mountain and Plateau
Basel is in the central plateau of
Switzerland, with cold and damp
winters similar to those in the Alps.

Average daily temperature (F)

month	min	max	monthly precipitation
Jan	26	36	2.9
April	40	59	3.0
July	56	76	5.4
Oct	43	57	3.0

all climate statistics from Fodor's World Weather Guide

Beyeler Foundation Museum

Riehen (Basel), Switzerland 1992-97
Renzo Piano Building Workshop

A MODERN ART MUSEUM, EXTREMELY ENERGY EFFICIENT DESPITE ITS ALL-GLASS ROOF, IN WHICH ARCHITECTURE AND NATURE ARE INTIMATELY INTERWOVEN IN A BUILDING NESTLED INTO ITS SETTING.

The Beyeler Foundation Museum is beautifully embedded in its place. Despite an all glass roof, it is exceptionally energy efficient, a condition achieved by precise engineering rather than any particularly innovative strategy. The result of a public/private partnership, the museum gives the public access to an exceptional private collection of modern art and is set in the park-like grounds of an historic villa that now houses the museum restaurant and offices. The museum is squeezed between the stone walls that edge the long sides of the site, and the generating motif of the plan, four long parallel walls, seems almost a direct consequence of these pressures.

Over these heavy, dark, earth-bound walls, clad in a stone resembling the local sandstone, floats a diaphanous roof of glass and steel shaded by rows of sloping panes of milky glass. These are the upper-most layers of a series of elements that control the admission of light. These include horizontal, automatically controlled louvers in a deep loft space sealed below by a glass ceiling above the galleries, and the panels of perforated steel that form the visible ceiling. This loft also forms a thermal buffer, reducing heat gains and losses. Adding further energy efficiencies is the displacement air-conditioning system that keeps conditions stable in the lower parts of the tall galleries occupied by paintings and people while allowing temperatures to fluctuate under the ceiling, where air is exhausted to pass through heat exchangers.

This is a subtly suggestive building. When first seen, end-on, rising from a pool, it seems to be a small, temple-like sanctuary for contemplating art. It is then revealed to be also a large, tunable machine that combines the provision of ideal light and humidity conditions with energy efficiency. It proves that achieving the latter is not incompatible with architecture of the very highest artistic standards in a building that marries in glorious harmony architecture, art, technology and nature.

For all its understatement, the design sets up a brilliant processional sequence of arrival at and movement through the museum. Entering through the street gates, the museum is first seen end-on, rising temple-like from its lily pond. An elongated lobby draws visitors towards the middle of the museum, the interior of which is a hybrid of elongated galleries and closed rooms linked in threes by enfilade views. The meandering route first turns back southwards to re-establish intimate contact with pond and garden. The west-facing winter garden with its elevated view over fields and hills is discovered later, providing a resting point and contrasting relationship with nature. A sunken portion of the winter garden gives access to the basement temporary exhibition gallery.

Below: The museum, whose long axis is oriented roughly north-south, is on the grounds of an historic villa housing its offices and restaurant at the southern end of the site. Screened by a stone boundary wall, the museum is barely noticeable from the street; its full extent is only seen from the fields to the west. A winter garden offers views over the fields and acts as a thermal buffer between the galleries and outside.

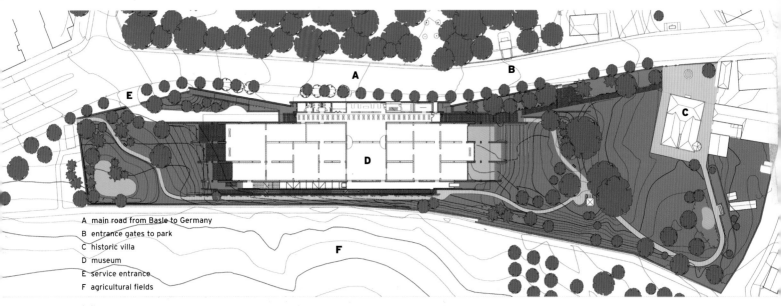

A main road from Basle to Germany
B entrance gates to park
C historic villa
D museum
E service entrance
F agricultural fields

Housing fragile art, the museum has to be air-conditioned, yet is exceptionally energy efficient. A product of precise rather than innovative engineering, this is achieved by a deep loft with various light-controlling devices, displacement air-conditioning with heat exchangers and the tall volume of the galleries. Air let in through the floor stratifies in layers of differing temperature to provide stable conditions where occupied by people and paintings, while temperatures vary considerably under the ceiling closing the loft.

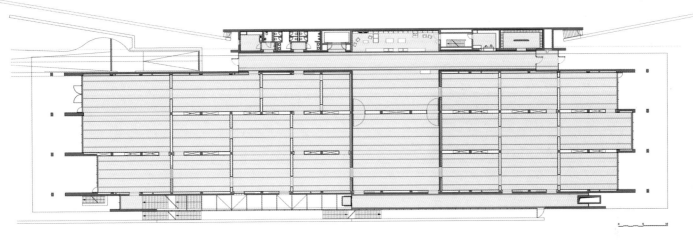

A elongated entrance lobby
B gallery
C glazed loft
D glass sunshade
E winter garden
F temporary exhibition gallery
G storage
H service access

The primary design intent was to provide ideal conditions for viewing art in natural light, which is alive to and changes with conditions outside for as much of every day as is possible. In Switzerland, this meant an entirely glazed roof, here shaded by sloping panes of tempered glass double-fritted solid white and held above the roof. To achieve the energy efficiency also insisted upon in Switzerland necessitated a deep glazed loft packed with further devices for controlling and diffusing the light. A strip of windows separates and heightens the contrast between roof and walls, and is shaded, like the big windows at the porch ends, by overhanging panes of fritted glass.

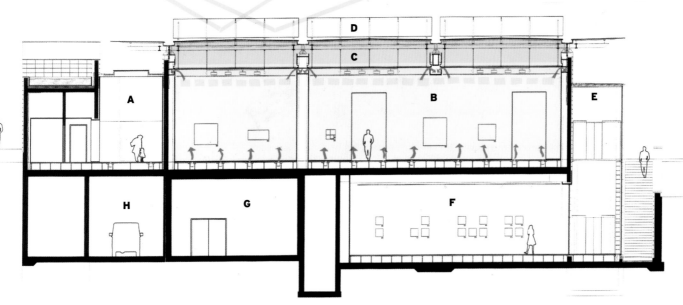

The intimate interweaving of architecture and nature is achieved particularly at the porch ends. Here elements of the building overhang and stop short of each other to achieve a complex interlocking with pond and park, whether viewed from inside or outside. Thus the roof projects over columns rising from the pond, which reaches inwards at the exact level of the gallery floor to extend its serenity inside. From the gallery, it is not only pond and park that are visible but also the parts of the building that intermesh with them.

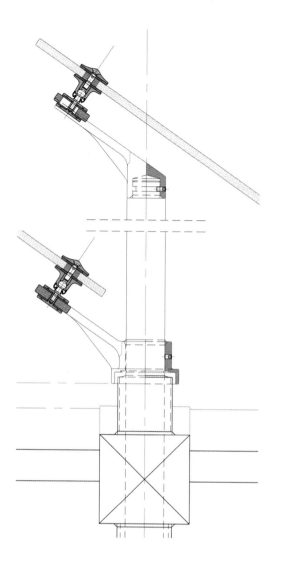

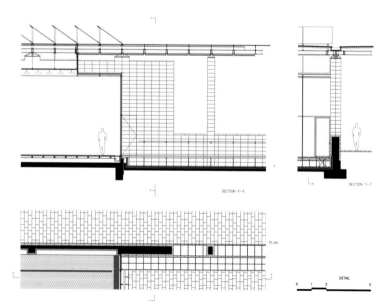

SECTION X-X

SECTION Y-Y

PLAN

DETAIL

0   1   2   5

This page: The roof and loft together form an adjustable mechanism to control and modulate the incoming light, the various elements propped or suspended off the steel structural grid. Frosted glass sunshades exclude direct sun; the roof excludes ultra-violet light; horizontal louvers adjust to control light intensity; and the glass ceiling, on which workmen can walk, seals the space so that it is a thermal buffer.

Opposite page top left: The design contrasts earth-bound, dark stone-faced walls with a floating, crisp yet diaphanous roof of white painted steel and frosted glass, detailed to emphasize the sense of lightness and outward projection. Consistent with this, a strip of glass separates the head of the wall from the structural grid.

Top right: View through the porch to the park.

Bottom: First view of the museum is the southern porch rising temple-like from its pond. Here all the elements of the building are made visible, and overlapped to heighten their distinctness from each other, in a single x-ray view. Thus physical transparency also becomes intellectual transparency of organizational concept and constructional principles.

Climate: Cool Temperate
Frankfurt am Main lies in the
lowland section of the Northern
Rhineland, with cold winters
and warm summers.

Average daily temperature (F):

month	min	max	monthly precipitation
Jan	29	38	2.3
April	42	60	1.7
July	58	77	2.8
Oct	44	58	2.1

1   low energy/ high performance

2   replenishable sources

5   long life, loose fit

7   embedded in place

8   access and urban context

9   health and happiness

Commerzbank Headquarters

Frankfurt, Germany 1991-1997
Foster and Partners

AN OFFICE TOWER IN DOWNTOWN FRANKFURT THAT REINVENTS THE SKYSCRAPER IN A STRUCTURE WITH A HOLLOW SHAFT AROUND WHICH SPIRAL SKY GARDENS THAT ARE INTRINSIC TO BOTH THE ENERGY-SAVING STRATEGY AND SOCIAL LIFE OF THE BUILDING.

The Commerzbank tower, the headquarters of one of Germany's major banks, radically reinvents the skyscraper. The conventional office tower has been cut open and turned inside out, so that the usual core of elevators, stairs and toilets is distributed to the corners of the triangular tower, leaving a hollow shaft around which spiral a series of sky gardens. Through these natural light and fresh air enter the hollow core and the offices that face in on it, thus bringing these to all parts of the building along with spectacular views, the close proximity of plants and the chance to socialize in the semi-outdoors.

A double-layered façade that intercepts the rain and breaks the force of the wind allows even the outer facing offices to be naturally ventilated. For most of the year the building relies on natural light and ventilation alone during daylight hours. In the heat of summer, offices are cooled by chilled ceilings and in winter receive perimeter heating. Only in the middle of these seasons is the building also automatically sealed and air-conditioned, but monitoring shows this to be for less than the thirty percent of the year initially predicted.

Energy efficiency is by no means the building's sole claim to greenness. It is responsive to its dual contexts of being both one of a cluster of towers and yet retains the street and cornice line of its setting. More importantly, the sky gardens, used for coffee, snacks and informal meetings, are part of a hierarchy of social foci, which include a communal space in the middle of each arm of offices and a lobby-level, covered plaza with restaurants used by both bank employees and public. Together these bring the social vibrancy and sense of community intrinsic to a fully green architecture.

Opposite page: Day and night views of the tower show how eight-floor high Vierendeel trusses supporting the column-free offices span between the corner circulation and service shafts, leaving between them the four floor high sky gardens that spiral around the tower.

Separated from its stone-faced neighbor by the tall new arcade, the base of the tower respects the traditional block pattern.

This page: The tallest building in Europe, the Commerzbank tower responds to its dual context. One of a cluster of towers, it also retains the street and cornice line of the traditional block pattern of the city-center area. The arcade leads to a glass-roofed public 'plaza' (below right) beside the lobby in the foot of the tower from which it is possible to look up the central shaft (below left).

Right: Ground floor plan.

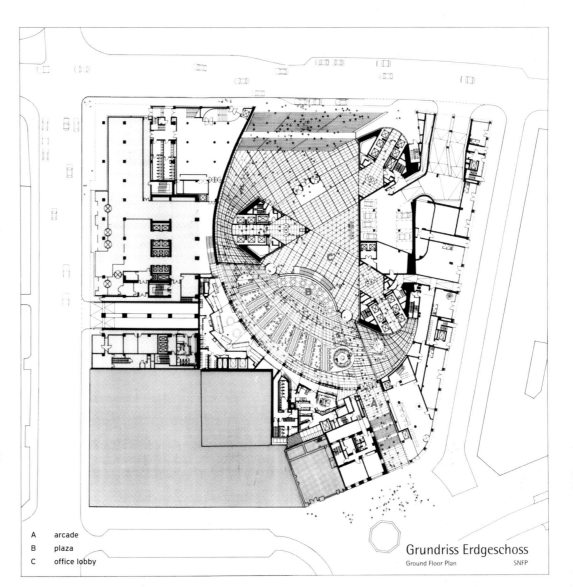

A   arcade
B   plaza
C   office lobby

Grundriss Erdgeschoss
Ground Floor Plan   SNFP

Right: The basic concept illustrated in the architect's sketches is of a three-sided tower with an open core around which offices are stacked to create the spiral of sky gardens which admit light and air to the central shaft and, together with the outer double façade, result in a tower that breathes without the aid of air-conditioning. At least two sky gardens can be seen from every desk overlooking the shaft, providing spectacular views and invitations to interact with colleagues. The design was thus inspired as much by the social as by the energy-saving intentions of the green agenda.

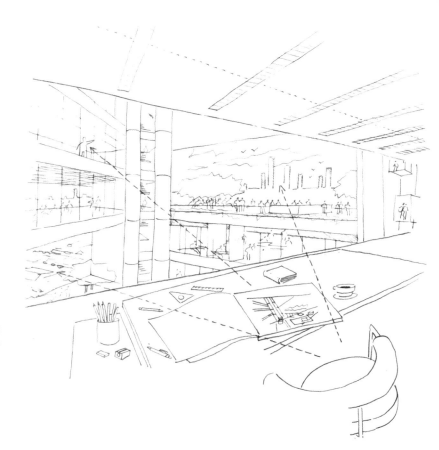

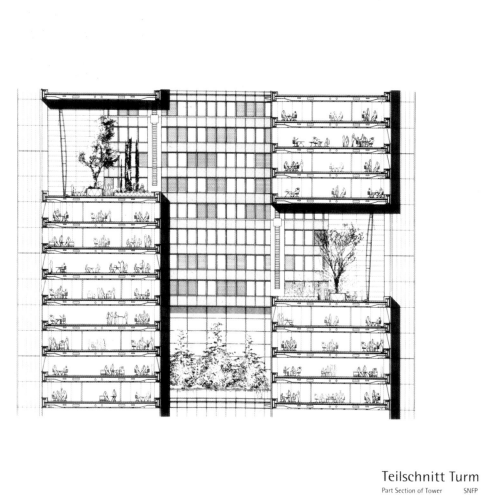

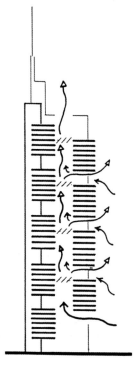

Teilschnitt Turm

Part Section of Tower   SNFP

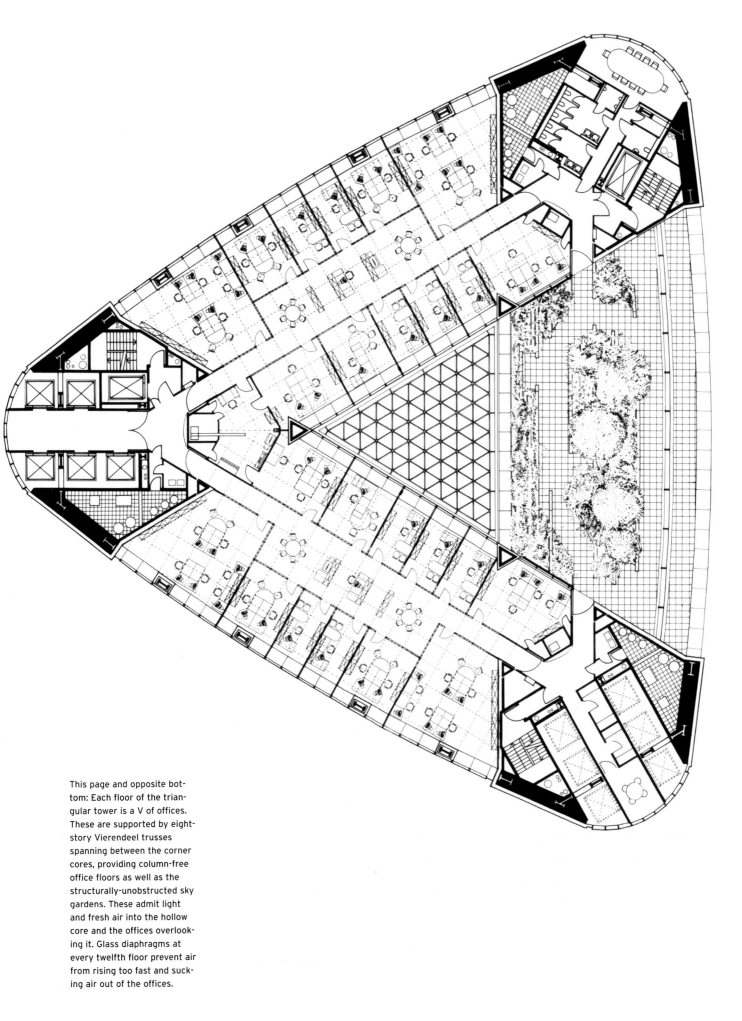

This page and opposite bottom: Each floor of the triangular tower is a V of offices. These are supported by eight-story Vierendeel trusses spanning between the corner cores, providing column-free office floors as well as the structurally-unobstructed sky gardens. These admit light and fresh air into the hollow core and the offices overlooking it. Glass diaphragms at every twelfth floor prevent air from rising too fast and sucking air out of the offices.

The building was designed in close collaboration with engineers: structural engineer Chris Wise of Ove Arup and Partners and mechanical engineers from Roger Preston and Partners. The latter analyzed and modeled conditions within and outside the building, extensively examining wind flows and air movement, temperature and pressure gradients, etc. in the atrium and offices.

This page, top: In summer the outer offices are naturally ventilated through windows in the inner layer of the double facade. The inner offices are ventilated by air drawn in through large windows in the glazed screens closing the sky gardens and exhausting through others higher up. On hot days the ceilings are chilled, and only in the peak of summer are office windows sealed and air-conditioning used.

Bottom: In winter the windows in the sky garden screens are partially closed to decrease the inlet of cold air. As temperatures drop, perimeter heating comes on in the offices. In very cold weather the offices are sealed and heated. The sky gardens always remain naturally ventilated and intermediate in temperature between the offices and outside.

Opposite page: Computer modelling of environmental impact and internal conditions; isometric of structural frame and details of opening windows in double-layered façade.

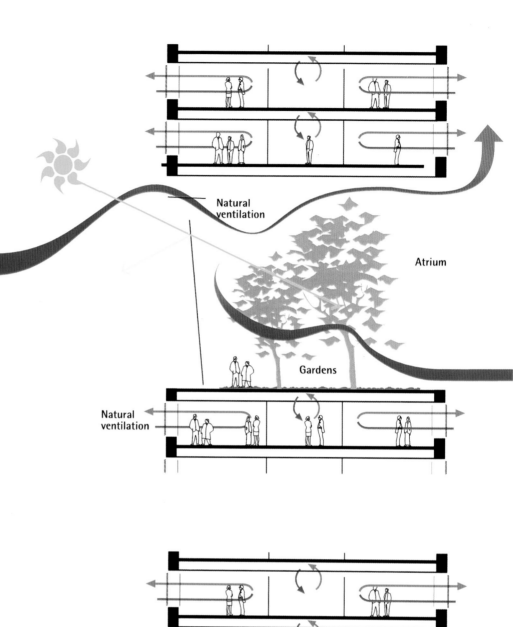

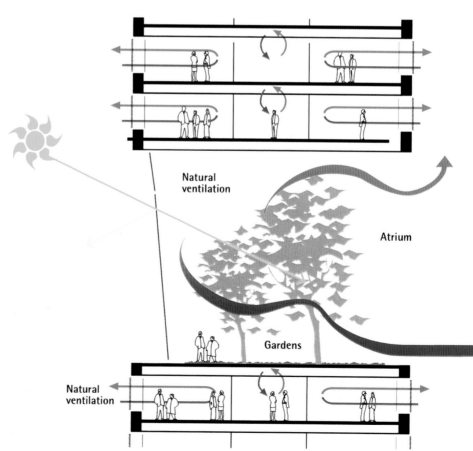

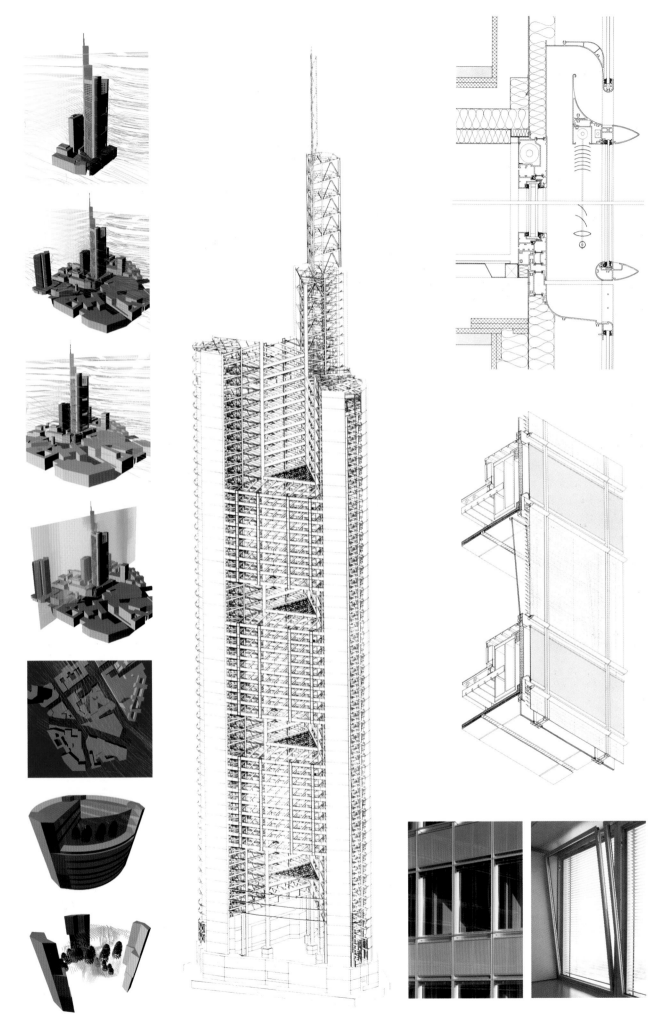

A key aspect of the design is that it creates a whole hier-archy of communal foci that foster social interaction and a sense of community. These include the communal space at the center of each office floor, the sky gardens shared by the floors immediately above and below them, and the lobby-level plaza.

Opposite page: The sky gardens, where people have informal meetings and take coffee and snacks, are the key elements in both the energy-saving strategy and social life of the building. They have a semi-outdoor climate, as the admission of air to the hollow core is controlled by the big pivoting windows in their four-floor high glazing. For variety and to aid orientation, sky gardens facing south have plants from the Mediterranean, those facing east have Japanese plants and west-facing gardens have American plants.

This page: The glass-roofed plaza has restaurants used by both bank employees and public. Commerzbank employees not only meet each other and members of the public here but also Commerzbank colleagues who work in an older tower directly adjacent the plaza.

Climate: Tropical
The Sunshine Coast of Queensland
has a tropical climate, with little
rain in winter and high temperatures
year-round.

Average daily temperature (F):

month	min	max	monthly precipitation
Jan	69	85	6.4
April	61	79	3.7
July	49	68	2.2
Oct	60	80	2.5

Cotton Tree Pilot Housing

Sunshine Coast, Queensland, Australia 1992-1994
Clare Design

A LOW-RISE MULTIFAMILY HOUSING DEVELOPMENT IN A SUBTROPI-
CAL CLIMATE THAT SERVES A MIXED COMMUNITY OF FAMILIES AND
SINGLE PEOPLE, HOMEOWNERS AND RENTERS, IN A COMPLEX THAT
PRESERVES TREES ON THE SITE AND DRAWS ON THE LOCAL VERNAC-
ULAR FOR ITS FORMS, MATERIALS, AND LOW ENERGY SOLUTIONS.

The Cotton Tree Housing started as a pilot project instigated by the Queensland government
'to investigate affordable housing that is socially, environmentally and aesthetically appropriate to the Sunshine Coast region.' It was realized as a mix of public housing (four three-bed-
room units with ground level access, a ground
floor disabled apartment and apartments for
singles above ground) and private houses (eight
family units). Careful design, drawing on the
local vernacular of beach houses and accumulated empirical experience, has resulted in homes
that require no air-conditioning in these subtropical climes. A substantial stand of paper-
bark trees was retained and sensitively integrated into the complex.

Site planning achieves a layering of inter-
mediary thresholds between public and private
to reach the units, and beyond these is often
another layered transition between private terrace and communal garden. The result is subtle
invitations to interaction with neighbors and the
formation of communal bonds. This arrangement, as well as the internal organization of the
units in plan and section, guides breezes across
the site and through the dwellings and linking
stairwells. The interiors are also kept cool by the
way the roofs overhang and shades project to
protect balconies and windows from the fierce
sun. Lightweight claddings shade the main walls
and draw ventilation up the cavity that separates
them from these walls. All this also leads to great
visual vivacity, enhanced by the lush vegetation
that is starting to assert its presence.

This page: The public housing is in the southern portion of the site, where a wall of units edges Kingsford South Parade and creates a gateway into the access motor court. The units have shaded balconies on the north while projecting roofs and shades protect windows on the south from early morning and late evening sun. Wooden slats let breezes through while providing privacy to balconies and street-facing bedroom and bathroom windows. The slat-screened garden in the photograph opens off a ground-level disabled apartment.

Opposite page: The northern part of the site is occupied by eight private houses. These are reached from a semi-public motor court off Hinkler Parade, from which semi-private paths and stairs lead to each house. The progression from street to houses to garden is shown by the photographs. These also show how the various constructional elements are expressed independently, casting shade, welcoming in the breezes and creating a lively, eminently livable aesthetic.

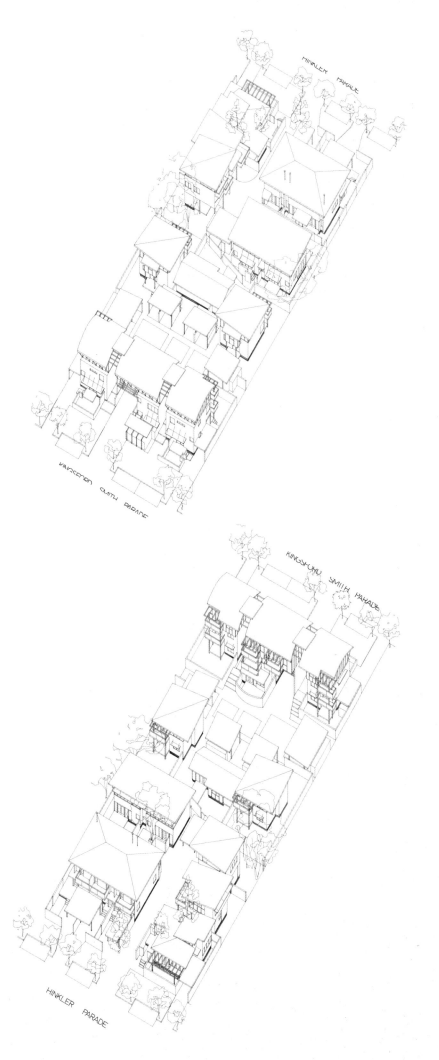

This page: The plans and sections of the units, like the site plan and communal stairwells, are designed to channel the breezes through them as well as allow flexibility in use and furnishing. Corrugated steel cladding is set forward of walls to shade them and create a cooling ventilated cavity.

Opposite page: To suit the context, close to the beach, as well as the climate of subtropical Queensland, the design draws on the local beach house vernacular of shaded porches and windows and light-weight construction with a low thermal inertia.

SECTION / EAST ELEVATION

Climate: Cool Temperate
Würzburg is in the Northern German
Plain, a low-lying, gently undulating
area that is an extension of the North
European Plain.

Average daily temperature (F):

month	min	max	monthly precipitation
Jan	26	35	1.8
April	39	56	1.7
July	57	75	2.9
Oct	42	56	1.9

1 low energy/ high performance

2 replenishable sources

5 long life, loose fit

6 total life cycle costing

9 health and happiness

10 community and connection

Götz Headquarters

Würzburg, Germany 1993-1995
Webler + Geissler Architekten

A MINIMALIST YET SOPHISTICATED AND SENSUAL OFFICE BLOCK, A GLASS BOX WITHIN A GLASS BOX, WRAPPED AROUND A PLANTED ATRIUM WITH AN OPERABLE ROOF AND MADE COMFORTABLY HABITABLE BY FLOWS OF AIR THROUGH THE OUTER CAVITY AND ATRIUM.

At first glance, the Götz building, the headquarters of a curtain-wall manufacturer, looks like a hermetically sealed and air-conditioned glass box, the most simplistic of building types that is typical of locations like this suburban industrial park site. Closer inspection shows it to be highly sophisticated in its carefully coordinated energy-saving strategies. The all-glass wall, adopted to admit maximum daylight, proves to be two skins of double glazing separated by a two-foot gap. Bringing more light into the center of the 133 x 133 foot block is a glass-roofed atrium.

Adjustable flaps opening to the outside at the top and bottom of the cavity between the glass walls, sliding doors and pivoting fanlights in the inner glass skin and motors that raise and slide aside the glass roof of the atrium are all used to adjust ventilation. Pivoting sunshades over the atrium roof control the admission of direct sunlight, while Venetian blinds in the wall cavity can be adjusted to admit or exclude direct sun, reflect it deep into the building or absorb its heat to warm the cavity. Fans in the corners of the cavity switch on to redistribute the warm air from the sunny to shaded faces of the building. All of these are adjusted to suit the season and time of day.

The building's many complementary heating, cooling, and ventilating systems are precisely coordinated by the building management system. Two hundred fifty sensors monitor a wide range of conditions measured throughout the interior, and also outside the building, and a computer compares these, using fuzzy logic and neural network systems, with past situations and the responses then made which are stored in its memory. In this way the building management system predicts with increasing accuracy how to best prepare the building to meet these conditions while providing optimal comfort conditions with minimal energy expenditure.

Yet these sophisticated systems account for only part of the building's significance and pleasantness as a workplace. Unlike so many glass boxes, this one is not only energy-efficient but also delivers inside the promise of abundant light, space and transparency. The generous ceiling heights and column spacings, minimalist detail and all-glass partitions and balustrades which almost disappear, all contribute immensely to these qualities. Adding a further dimension is the atrium, the visual and social focus of the building, with its planting and pool.

Every element of the building contributes to climate control, and all can be adjusted to work in several independent or coordinated ways. Thus in summer, the inner skin of the ventilated double wall opens up, as does the roof of the atrium whose pond and plants cool and humidify the air as well as provide a pleasant visual and social focus to the light and spacious offices. On hot days ceiling panels are chilled by cold water. If necessary in cold snaps, these same panels can use hot water to warm the space before the slower-response under-floor radiant heating (also hot water) becomes effective. In such weather heat exchangers recover warmth from exhaust air.

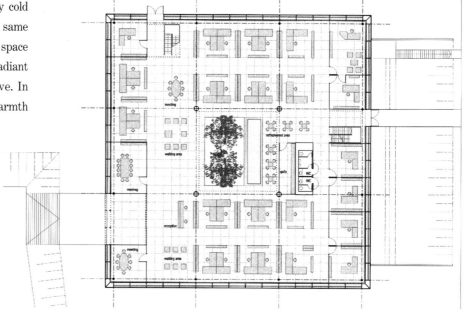

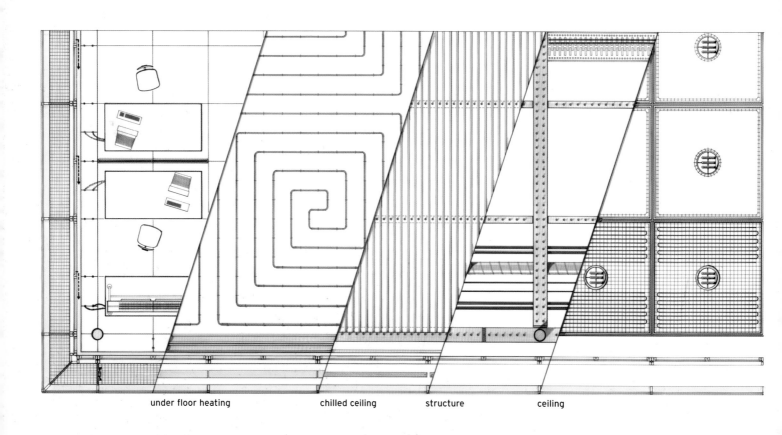

under floor heating   chilled ceiling   structure   ceiling

This page: Ventilation in the cavity between the glass walls is controlled by flaps at its top and bottom and by fans in its corners. In winter the cavity is sealed and the Venetian blinds are set to expose heat-absorbent surfaces, thus warming the cavity. The fans then blow warmed air from the building's sunny sides to the shaded sides. This ensures that the whole building is cozily jacketed by warm air.

Opposite page, top and middle: In summer the wall cavity is ventilated at top and bottom, and the inner wall and atrium roof opened up. These can safely remain open at night to purge excess heat from the structure. The Venetian blinds in the cavity are set to exclude sun (as are sun-control elements above the atrium roof) or reflect light onto the ceiling and deep into the offices. If temperatures rise, heat from 2,000 square feet of roof-top solar panels drives an absorption cooling plant to provide cold water for chilled ceiling panels.

Bottom: In winter the wall cavity is sealed top and bottom and the Venetian blinds are set so that the upper portion admits the warming sun to fall on the floor while the lower portion exposes a heat-absorbent surface to warm the cavity. Hot water from the solar collectors provides radiant under floor heating. Only after prolonged sunless periods of below freezing external temperatures is supplementary heat needed from a gas-fired boiler.

Summer day

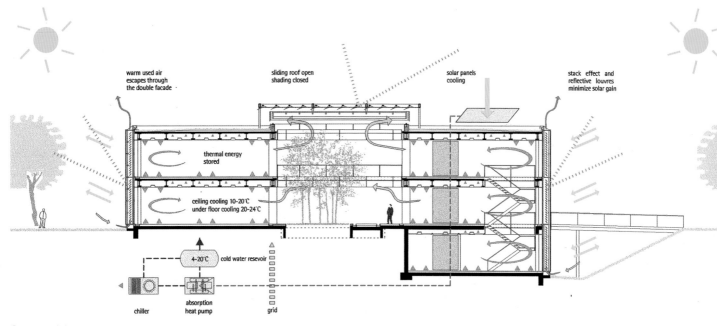

warm used air escapes through the double facade

sliding roof open shading closed

solar panels cooling

stack effect and reflective louvres minimize solar gain

thermal energy stored

ceiling cooling 10-20°C under floor cooling 20-24°C

4-20°C   cold water resevoir

chiller

absorption heat pump

grid

Summer night

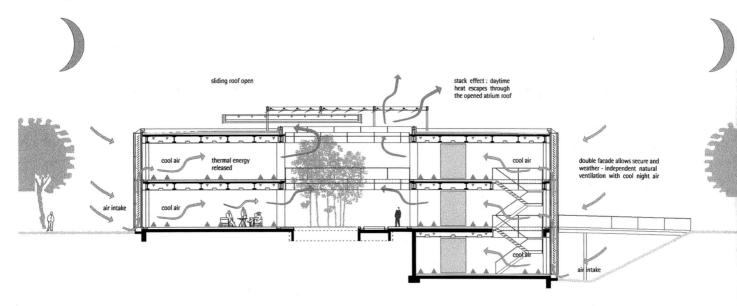

sliding roof open

stack effect : daytime heat escapes through the opened atrium roof

cool air   thermal energy released

cool air

air intake

cool air

cool air

double facade allows secure and weather - independent natural ventilation with cool night air

cool air

air intake

Sunny winter's day

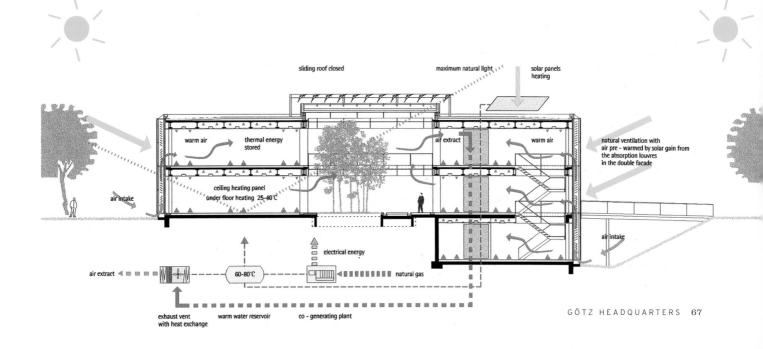

sliding roof closed

maximum natural light

solar panels heating

warm air   thermal energy stored

air extract

warm air

ceiling heating panel under floor heating 25-40°C

air intake

natural ventilation with air pre - warmed by solar gain from the absorption louvres in the double facade

air intake

electrical energy

air extract

60-80°C

natural gas

exhaust vent with heat exchange

warm water reservoir

co - generating plant

Climate: Cool Temperate
Hanover is in the North German
Plain, a low-lying, gently undulating
area that is an extension of the
North European Plain.

Average daily temperature (F):

month	min	max	monthly precipitation
Jan	28	37	1.8
April	38	56	1.9
July	55	73	3.1
Oct	42	56	2.2

Hall 26

Hanover, Germany 1994-1996
Herzog + Partner

A LARGE EXHIBITION HALL WITH A LONGITUDINAL SECTION THAT EXACTLY MARRIES STRUCTURAL EFFICIENCY AND SPEED OF ERECTION WITH IDEAL CONDITIONS OF NATURAL LIGHT AND VENTILATION.

Hall 26 is an exhibition hall in the grounds of the international trade fair outside Hanover, Germany. The challenge facing the architect was to design a vast structure which would accommodate yet discipline more or less any collection of exhibits, be built very fast between trade shows and yet also be a model of energy-efficiency. For speed of construction, a suspended structure was adopted, with the roof sagging between tall trestle masts that were prefabricated, then transported to the site to be quickly pinned to their footings and hoisted into position. Energy efficiency necessitated making maximum use of natural light as well as of convection currents and the Venturi effect to exhaust air that is pumped in mechanically. A triumph of the design is how it so exactly marries these concerns, the structural arrangement and resulting longitudinal section matching precisely the profiles needed for light and ventilation. The big gestures in this building—the swooping roofs, supporting trestles and vast expanses of glass—are beautifully offset by smaller-scale, visually crisp repetitive details that give more precise definition and scale to the scheme.

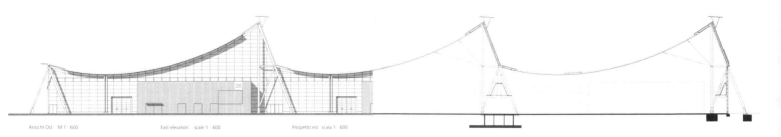

Ansicht Ost   M 1 : 600   East elevation   scale 1 : 600   Prospetto est   scala 1 : 600

Opposite page: Hall 26 stands out from its neighbors, some of which also achieve their visual identity from their dominant long-span structures. The building is a simple rectangle in plan, and is glazed on all sides except where service blocks are set into the ends of each structural bay. These service blocks house lavatories, storerooms and plant rooms.

This page: The big gestures—the swooping roofs, supporting trestles, and vast expanses of glass—are offset by smaller-scale, visually crisp repetitive details that give more precise definition and scale to the forms. Among the best examples of such details are the brackets that support the head of the glazing on the long elevations and project out under the eaves. Similarly, the fixed louvered sunshades break down the scale of the south elevation (on which the 26 is emblazoned).

This page: The structural section results in a series of tall north-facing clerestories admitting abundant natural light, which is reflected down off the underside of the roof. Polished steel strips stuck to the structural sandwich-panel ceiling bounce downwards both the daylight and artificial light from uplighters. More natural light enters the building's glazed sides and roof lights near where the roofs sag lowest. These are glazed in a sandwich panel, invented earlier by the architect, which admits all light except direct shafts from the sun.

The structure was designed for speed of erection. Rows of trestle masts, three reaching nearly 100 feet high with a fourth lower row, were prefabricated offsite, then pinned to footings in rows 180 feet apart and hoisted into place. Flat steel bars, 12 inches wide and one and a half inches deep, were slung between these to support sandwich panels of two layers of wood separated by gravel. The heavy gravel ensures the roof's correct curve and, with cables from the masts to the steel bars, prevents uplift.

Opposite page: Fresh air is pumped in, from plant rooms at the ends of the structural bays, through triangular glass-sided ducts suspended between the legs of the trestles. The air rises by convection guided by the roof's rising curves towards the clerestories. Here the upward movement of air is reinforced by both stack and Venturi effects to exhaust through the head of the clerestories. The Venturi effect is aided by spoilers, like gigantic versions of those on racing cars, which cap the clerestories to channel the air.

1 fixed steel louvers shading
   south-facing glazing

2,3,4 roof lights with sandwich
   glazing excluding direct sun

5 wind spoiler

6 clear-glazed clerestory

10 glass-sided inlet air duct

11 space reserved for circulation

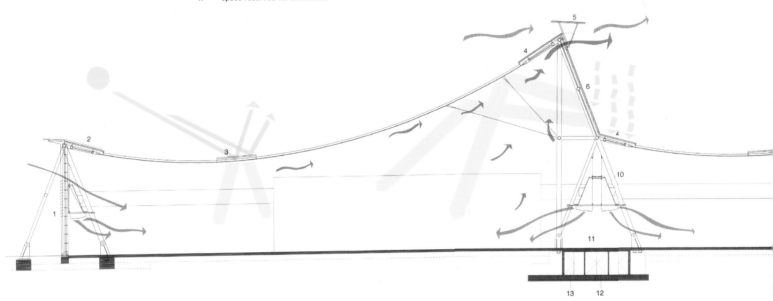

Climate: Cool Temperate
Nottingham lies in central England,
where the weather is generally
cool to mild with frequent clouds
and rain.

Average daily temperature (F)

month	min	max	monthly precipitation
Jan	35	42	3.0
April	40	54	2.1
July	54	68	2.7
Oct	45	55	2.7

Jubilee Campus, University of Nottingham

Nottingham, England 1996-1999

Michael Hopkins and Partners

INDUSTRIAL LAND HAS BEEN RECLAIMED IN A PROJECT IN WHICH ARCHITECTURE AND LANDSCAPING, SUN AND WIND, AND AN INGENIOUS ENVIRONMENTAL STRATEGY WORK TOGETHER TO PRODUCE EXTREMELY PLEASANT CONDITIONS FOR STUDY AND SOCIALIZING.

The Jubilee Campus extension of Nottingham University is a milestone in green architecture. It pioneers an innovative strategy, a combination of mechanical and wind-driven ventilation, as well as bringing together a wide range of other green strategies. Despite starting with an industrial 'brownfield' site, the buildings are now embedded in verdant nature. More than that, the landscaping, the architecture and its environmental systems are intimately fused into a single formal and functional whole. The landscaping is an intrinsic part of the architectural environmental systems: it filters and cools the air approaching the buildings, and even extends onto the roofs to improve insulation and prevent the build-up of reflected heat. It also purifies the water running off roofs, roads and parking areas.

The most conspicuously placed and shaped formal elements of the architecture, which is otherwise low-key and generic (and should prove immensely adaptable in the long term), are those that harness the wind to drive the internal ventilation systems. The buildings themselves are linked by a lakeside arcade, off which open the atria that connect classroom buildings. In addition to serving energy-saving functions the atria are, with the arcade, the main social spaces of the campus, which is also green in its social conviviality.

It is significant that the campus is not out of town but within easy walking distance of the main campus and well served by public transport. In urban terms it defines an edge and buffer between the bigger buildings of the town center and the suburban houses beyond the lake, situating the scheme in place as well as nature. All the above has been achieved with buildings that cost only $105 per square foot. This proves that even architecture that exemplifies all ten shades of green need cost no more than conventional buildings, yet will bring huge cost savings in the long term.

1 low energy/ high performance

2 replenishable sources

3 recycling: eliminating waste and pollution

4 embodied energy

5 long life, loose fit

6 total life cycle costing

7 embedded in place

8 access and urban context

9 health and happiness

10 community and connection

This page: Site plan.

Opposite page: The site, half a mile from the lushly landscaped main campus, was covered by factories. Where a stream ran before is now a lake edged by trees. These cool and filter the prevailing wind that drives the ventilation system of the new buildings lining the other side of the lake, where they are linked by a lake-side arcade. Lake and landscape also shelter wildlife, while reed beds purify rainwater run-off. The landscaping extends to the planted roofs of the academic blocks. As now developed the site makes an apt transition between the large buildings of the town center and the suburban housing beyond the lake.

The brick-faced blocks near the entrances to the site are student residences. The academic buildings are wood-clad. Projecting into the lake is the library, which spirals up as an inverted truncated cone on axis with a stack of auditoria. These auditoria intrude into one of the glass-roofed atria that separate the wings of the typical academic buildings that are the focus of the following pages.

Key

1 Lake
2 Grassed Island
3 Post Graduate Hall
4 Business School
5 Central Teaching Facility
6 Learning Resource Centre
7 Department of Computer Science
8 Central Catering Facility
9 Departments of Education and
  Continuing Education
10 Undergraduate Hall A
11 Undergraduate Hall B
12 Entrance
13 Main Entrance

30m

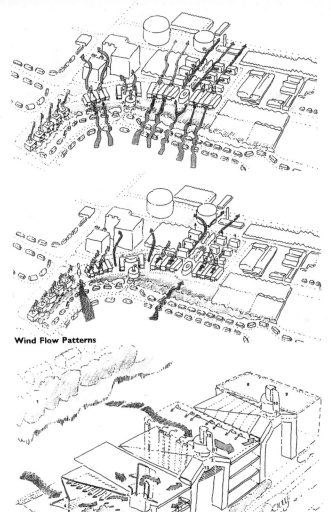

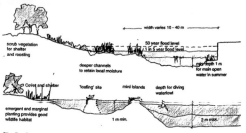

Summer Flow Over the Campus

Prevailing wind flows over lake, cooling air before it enters the buildings

Block spacing allows good natural ventilation

Atrium front acts as wind catcher, providing wind assisted ventilation in summer

Rear face of atrium open, bypassing impedance of turret

scrub vegetation for shelter and roosting

50 year flood level
1 in 5 year flood level

min depth 1 m for main open water in summer

deeper channels to retain local moisture

Coves and shelter
'loafing' site
mini islands
depth for diving waterfowl

emergent and marginal planting provides good wildlife habitat

1 m min.
2 m max

Site Sections

Winter Flow Over the Campus

Linear existing woodland thickened to provide wildlife haven and shelter belt

Rotating turrets catch wind jar fresh air supply at the same time as exhausting air for extract. This device allows for simple air to air heat recovery and controlled internal ventilation, with fans cutting in only as wind pressures drop

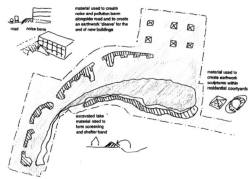

material used to create noise and pollution berm alongside road and to create an earthwork 'sleeve' for the end of new buildings

road
noise berm

material used to create earthwork sculptures within residential courtyards

excavated lake material used to form screening and shelter band

Land Balance

Wind Flow Patterns

1. Existing woodland reinforced to provide shade and some cooling
2. Heat Recovery Unit enables 100% fresh air supply with 60% heat recycled from exhaust airstream
3. Prevailing wind cooled by lake surface
4. Front face of atrium channels wind to increase summer ventilation rate - glass louvres control air flow
5. Shade and evaporative cooling from atrium planting
6. Container planting sanitises irrigating grey water from cloakrooms
7. Blackwater output to 'Clivus' type composting units or the 'living machine'
8. Additional Photovoltaic panels can be mounted on flat roof in the future
9. Evaporative cooling from turf roof cools top floor in summer
10. Tracking windvane
11. Heat recovery unit

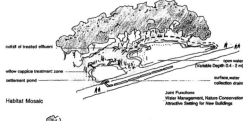

outfall of treated effluent

willow coppice treatment zone
settlement pond

open water (Variable Depth 0.4 - 2 m)

surface water collection drain

Habitat Mosaic

Joint Functions
Water Management, Nature Conservation
Attractive Setting for New Buildings

Winter

Both fresh air intake and exhaust air through rotating wind turret enables heat recovery, and the opportunity for wind assisted ventilation.

Slow moving propellar fans (12) cut in as wind speed drops.

A water to air heat exchanger (13), supplied by the combined heat and power unit, preheats incoming fresh air before it is ducted into raised floor plenums (14), and reaches rooms through floor outlets.

Air rises vertically through displacement ventilation, warmed by occupancy and machines, to be extracted by facade ducts into a roof plenum discharging into the wind turret.

Summer

Air Supply to atrium maximised by opening all louvres at front and rear, bypassing wind turret.
Office Floors notionally ventilated to outside with night time pre-cooling.

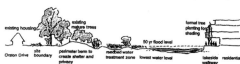

existing housing
existing mature trees

formal tree planting for shading

Orston Drive
site boundary

perimeter berm to create shelter and privacy

reedbed water treatment zone

50 yr flood level

lowest water level

lakeside residential walkway

Typical Section Through Lake Showing Potential Habitat Structure

Landscape

Environmental Strategy for Typical Academic Building

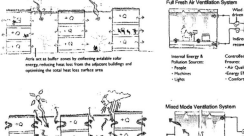

Full Fresh Air Ventilation System

Wind or fan driven system

Indirect heat recovery

Atria act as buffer zones by collecting available solar energy, reducing heat loss from the adjacent buildings and optimising the total heat loss surface area

Internal Energy & Pollution Sources:
• People
• Machines
• Lights

Controlled Ventilation Ensures:
• Air Quality
• Energy Efficiency
• Comfort

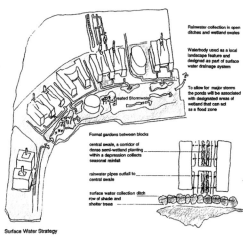

Rainwater collection in open ditches and wetland swales

Waterbody used as a local landscape feature and designed as part of surface water drainage system

To allow for major storms the ponds will be associated with designated areas of wetland that can act as a flood zone

treated Stormwater

Formal gardens between blocks

central swale, a corridor of dense semi-wetland planting within a depression collects seasonal rainfall

rainwater pipes outfall to central swale

surface water collection ditch
row of shade and shelter trees

Surface Water Strategy

Mixed Mode Ventilation System

Atria act as buffer zones providing shelter from wind and rain and increasing the period that natural ventilation can be allowed without creating cold draughts.

Opening windows provide greater fresh air rates and can purge heat & toxins as required.

Controlled ventilation is maintained as required by the occupants.

Winter: 30% of year

Cold Ambient Conditions
Controlled ventilation is essential in maintaining internal air quality, reducing uncontrollable heat losses (by opening windows), and to enable heat to be recovered from the internal energy sources which are an inherent part of the building function.

Mid-Season: 60% of year

Mild / Temperate Ambient Conditions
Natural ventilation can be allowed without upsetting the energy balance of the building. The atria act as climatic buffers to prolong the period of time that natural ventilation can be tolerated.

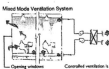

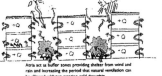

Full passive Ventilation System

Diurnal Cycle

Atria are naturally ventilated to prevent overheating - driven by buoyancy and external wind pressure.
Planting provides shade to the occupied level, solar gain is taken out by the 'canopy', low level surface temperatures remain low and stable. Water features provide local cooling & irrigation.

Night time purging of building precools the structure at the height of summer.

Controlled mechanical ventilation maintains air quality whilst making the most of the structure's thermal inertia.

Atrium Ventilation

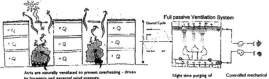

Summer: 10% of year

Warm, Moist Ambient Conditions
Controlled mechanical ventilation ensures fresh air distribution is maintained whilst gaining maximum benefit of the thermal inertia of the structure. The bottom of the atria is a cool shaded retreat, protected by irrigated planting and water features.
Occupants will learn that internal conditions will remain stable when windows are kept closed on the warmest days.
Evaporative cooling from green room.

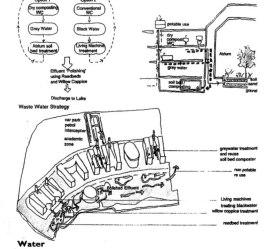

Residential Blocks

Option 1
Dry composting WC → Grey Water → Atrium soil bed treatment

Option 2
Conventional WC → Black Water → Living Machine treatment

Effluent 'Polishing' using Reedbeds and Willow Coppice

Discharge to Lake

potable use

dry compost WC
Atrium
grey water
soil bed composting
soil sand gravel

Waste Water Strategy

Energy Efficiency

Waste water is discharged into the local sewer where it can be properly dealt with. Collection of 'grey water' from buildings is not economically viable or practical in our climate as treatment is almost as onerous as that of 'black water.' Collection of rainwater should provide all the water resources the site requires.

Power, Heat and any cooling requirements are provided by a site combined heat and power system with heating backed up by Nottingham's District Heating system which runs off waste incineration.

Local Solar panels (up to 80% efficient) and PVcells (embodied energy payback <4 years) can be integrated into each building as necessary to suit each function, eg. hot water generation is appropriate for accommodation blocks, PV cells for teaching and office areas.

car park
petrol interceptor
academic zone

greywater treatment and reuse
soil bed composter

non potable re use

Living machines treating blackwater
willow coppice treatment

reedbed treatment

Polished Effluent

Water

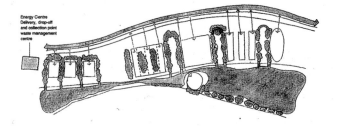

Energy Centre
Delivery, drop-off and collection point
waste management centre

Opposite page: As evidenced by the competition board, this design, like that of most innovative green buildings, was a close collaboration between architects and engineers. Here the latter were Ove Arup and Partners. The landscape design is by Battle McCarthy (who are also renowned for their green engineering).

This page: The main social spaces, which offer students ample opportunities to meet and interact in pleasant conditions, are the lake-side arcade that links all the buildings and the atria between the wings of each building. The largest of these atria, which are also intrinsic to the energy-saving strategy, houses the main campus cafeteria.

The typical academic building
consists of wings of rooms
separated by atria that serve
as thermal buffers between
inside and out. The atria are
naturally ventilated, drawing
air in through their scoop-
shaped lake fronts and
exhausting it on either side of
the stair towers. With their
plant rooms capped by rotating wind cowls, these are
major elements in the wind-
driven, mechanically-aided
ventilation system of the academic rooms. The cedar
cladding (from sustainably
managed forests) was chosen
as a replenishable material
of low-embodied energy,
and galvanized rather than
stainless steel is used
throughout because it is lower
in embodied energy and
less polluting to manufacture.

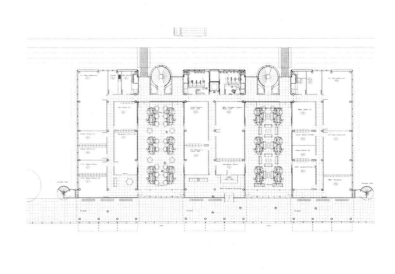

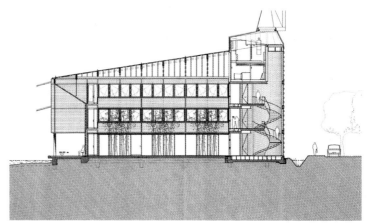

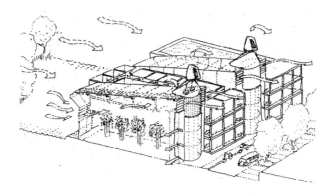

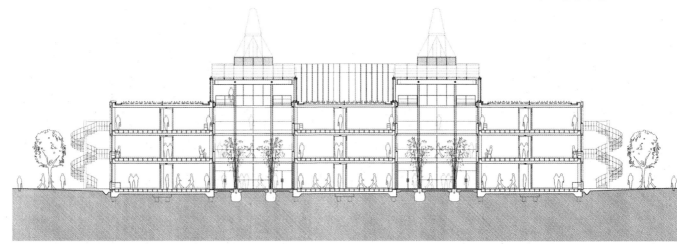

Although the incoming air is assisted by electric fans, the air is primarily drawn through the building (from plant rooms, down ducts flanking the stair shafts, under floors, through academic rooms and back along corridors and up the stair shafts) by suction due to the negative pressure created by the tracking wind cowls. (On still days, this expulsion of air is also assisted by fans – but these are usually the same days that the photovoltaic cells are generating the most electricity.) The key to the smooth functioning of such a system is to achieve minimal resistance to air movement within the system, and so minimal pressure drop throughout it. Yet, for all the sophistication of the ventilation systems, one of the most effective energy saving elements remains the simple device of exposing the concrete structure, particularly as ceilings, to exploit the temperature stabilizing effects of its considerable thermal inertia.

This page: The diagrams show the functioning of the plant rooms over the stair towers and below the wind cowls. The fans, heat exchange wheel, evaporative cooler and lou-vered dampers that switch air through bypasses work in four primary modes according to season and time of day. In peak summer conditions it is the exhaust air that is cooled before passing through the heat exchange wheel. In this way incoming air is cooled without humidification.

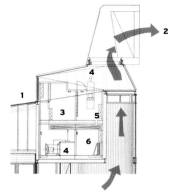

1	air intake
2	tracking cowl exhaust
3	heat exchange wheel
4	far
5	adjustable louvers
6	evaporative cooler

temperate weather; natural ventilation only

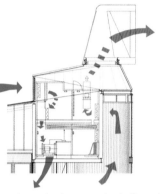

spring and autumn; mechanically ventilated

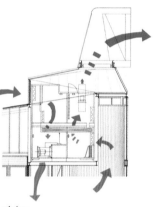

winter

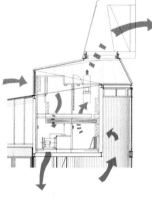

summer

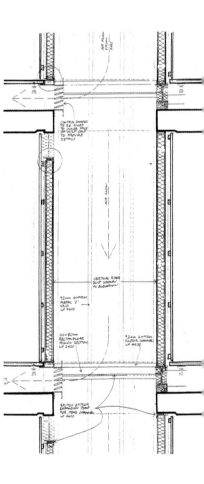

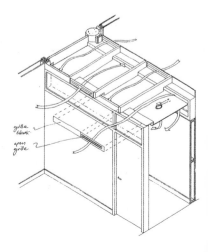

summer peak

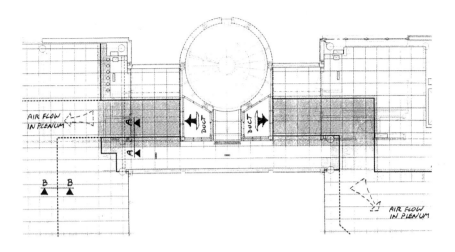

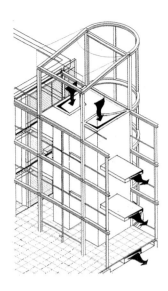

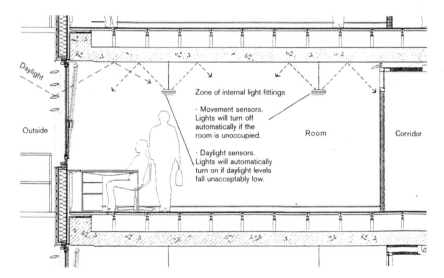

Zone of internal light fittings

- Movement sensors. Lights will turn off automatically if the room is unoccupied.

- Daylight sensors. Lights will automatically turn on if daylight levels fall unacceptably low.

Daylight

Outside

Room

Corridor

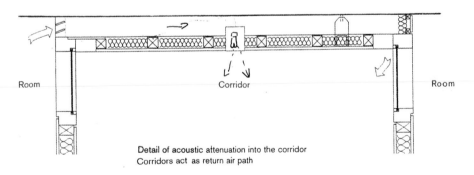

Detail of acoustic attenuation into the corridor
Corridors act as return air path

Room

Corridor

Room

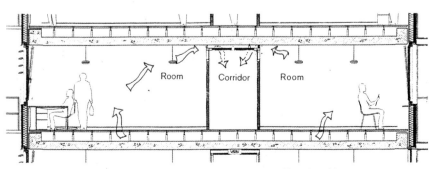

Section through Typical faculty building block showing position of corridor

The academic rooms are naturally ventilated for much of the year and ventilated by the wind-driven mechanical ventilation system during hot and cold periods. To be driven by the wind, with assistance from only low-powered fans, the whole ventilation system is designed to entail minimal friction and pressure drop. Intake air is admitted just below the exhaust cowls and blown down big ducts on either side of the stair shafts. From here it is guided into under-floor plenums from where it enters into the rooms. It is then drawn out over sound absorptive material above the corridors (so as not to compromise aural privacy) before descending into the corridor. The air is sucked back along the corridor to the stair shaft and up and out by the wind blowing past the cowl. On hot still days when there is insufficient wind to drive the system, photovoltaic cells shading the atria roof provide the electricity (indirectly, since it is fed into the national grid) to drive extract fans. Wooden louvers exclude direct sun, while their white upper surfaces reflect light deep into the rooms. Nighttime lighting is by high-efficiency fixtures that provide up and down lighting from the same light source.

Climate: Cool Temperate
Utrecht lies slightly inland from
the Dutch coast, with mild weather
tempered by the sea.

Average daily temperature (F):

month	min	max	monthly precipitation
Jan	31	40	2.7
April	40	56	1.9
July	55	72	3.0
Oct	44	57	2.8

Minnaert Building

Utrecht, The Netherlands 1994-97
Neutelings Riedijk Architecten

A MULTIFUNCTIONAL ACADEMIC BUILDING AS A PROVOCATIVE MANIFESTO: RAINWATER POURS THROUGH ROOFLIGHTS INTO A SHALLOW BASIN IN THE CENTRAL HALL, FROM WHICH IT IS PUMPED AROUND THE BUILDING TO CONDUCT AWAY THE HEAT GIVEN OFF BY LABORATORIES FULL OF COMPUTERS.

Rainwater pours through the roof of the Minnaert Building on the Uithof campus extension of the University of Utrecht to cascade noisily into a 150 by 30 foot basin filling half the building's cavernous central hall. This is on the second floor main circulation level, at which the building is connected by bridges to its neighbors. The water in the pool feeds a circulatory system by which the temperatures are controlled throughout the building, which houses facilities for three departments, including that of geophysics, and a restaurant serving the entire northwestern corner of the campus.

The original program for the building consisted of a detailed schedule of spaces plus a percentage extra for circulation, services and 'architecture.' The architects decided to concentrate all this space in the unasked-for central hall and to use the hall for a dramatically novel form of energy-efficient climatic control. With its laboratories and library packed with computers, the building needs no extra heating, even in the extremes of winter. Instead its spaces are cooled, and heat is conducted away from them, by circulating the rainwater through panels suspended below the ceilings. To prevent the water becoming too warm to serve this function in summer, it is pumped onto the roof to be cooled by the night air before plunging back into the pool. Rising and falling levels of water in the pool are emphasized by the sloping 'beach' which connects the bottom of the pool with the floor of the hall.

Construction consists of pre-cast, ochre-pigmented concrete slabs. Those forming the roof are suspended below pre-cast beams. (The steel mullions of strip windows and letters spelling MINNAERT are structural too.) Insulation is external to the concrete units, and the elevations are clad outside of this with a rough, rust-colored sprayed concrete. This is intended to emphasize the monolithic character of construction inside while also being 'wrinkled' to express that it is only a skin. Rather resembling an upward extrusion of earth, the effect seems appropriate to a department of geophysics.

Above: Approach from the center of the campus is towards the southeast corner. Here a deep loggia accommodates bicycles behind large letters announcing the building's name. Like the mullions of the strip window above, these are structural.

The building is assembled from ochre-pigmented pre-cast concrete slabs. Insulation is external to this. The outer cladding is intended to reassert the monolithic character of the construction while also clearly expressing its skin-like quality, hence the sprayed concrete and the elephantine wrinkles.

The design compresses contrast and variety into a rectangular envelope. Within this, each major space on the dominant second floor, from which bridges link to neighboring buildings, has its own distinct character. Most distinctive of all is the central hall from which all other spaces are accessed. A large part of this is given over to a pool filled with rainwater admitted through the roof. This water is circulated through panels suspended below the ceilings on the floor below to conduct away the heat from the computers in these laboratories.

If the water in the tank threatens to become too warm to do this effectively, it is pumped onto the roof at night to surrender its heat to the cold air before draining back into the tank.

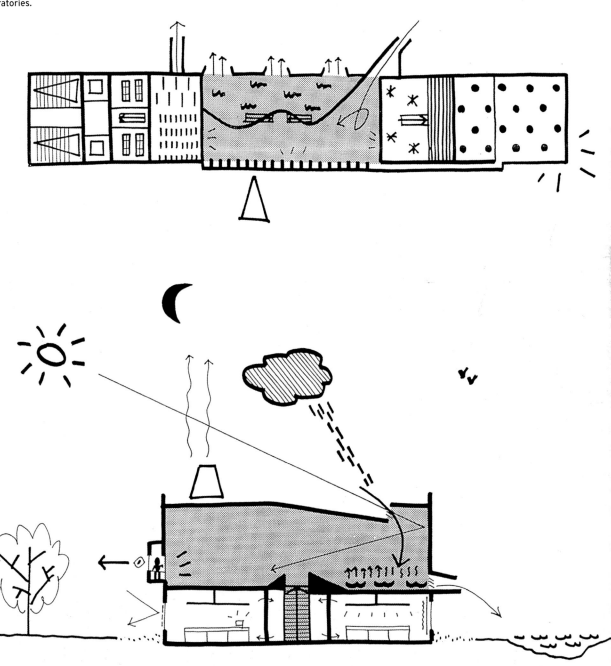

The design was devised to
achieve considerable spatial
and experiential contrast
within an overall compactness
of outer envelope and circulation. Hence the main spaces
are accessed from the central
hall and are each of distinct
and contrasting character.

Right: Section through
central hall and ground floor
laboratories.

Below: Second floor plan.

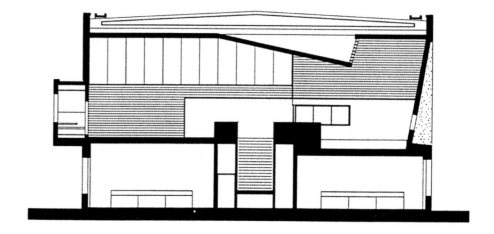

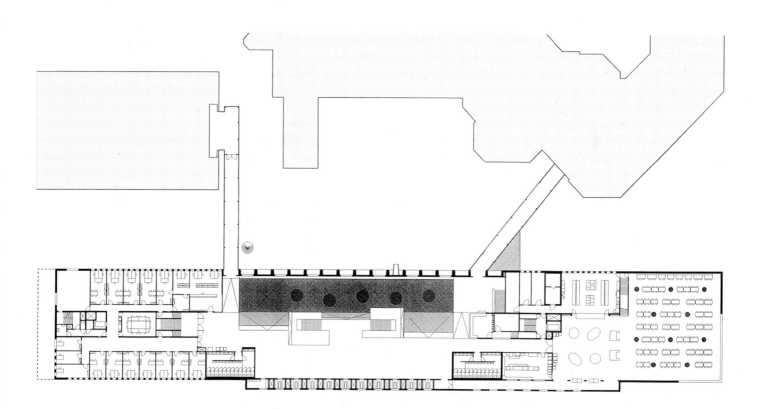

Top: The central hall contrasts the gloomy, clammy humidity of its main volume, and its echoing hard surfaces, with the brightly-lit, red-upholstered coziness of the conversation booths and their intimate scale and soft, sound-absorbing surfaces. The pool and the sloping wall beside it are finished in the same grey terrazzo as the floor of the hall and the plinths into which stairs descend. The opposite long wall and ceiling expose the ochre-pigmented pre-cast concrete slabs from which the building is constructed.

Middle: The library ceiling slopes down to a strip of glazing overlooking the central hall. The ceiling is lined with acoustic tiles painted blue, but with the randomly-spaced holes remaining white. The light, sectional shape and star-like ceiling pattern create a suitably contemplative space.

Bottom: The cafeteria is on two levels, with a gallery overlooking the main double height space and opening onto its own walled-in rooftop terrace. Besides articulating and animating the space, the non-structural columns serve other functions. The top portion provides light, from domed roof lights above them and artificial lights within, while the lower portions conceal electronic speakers.

Climate: Cool Temperate
Herne-Sodingen lies in the Ruhr
industrial region of North Rhine-
Westphalia.

Average daily temperature (F):

month	min	max	monthly precipitation
Jan	30	39	2.4
April	41	57	2.4
July	57	75	2.7
Oct	45	57	2.1

Mont-Cenis Training Center

Herne-Sodingen, Germany 1991-1999
Jourda & Perraudin Architectes, Jourda Architectes,
Hegger Hegger Schleiff Planer + Architekten

A LARGE GLASS BOX WITH INTERNAL WOODEN STRUCTURE CREATES A MICROCLIMATE AND NEW PUBLIC SPACE IN A FACILITY THAT BRINGS EMPLOYMENT, EDUCATION AND CIVIC FUNCTIONS TO A RECLAIMED MINING SITE IN THE RUHR REGION.

The Mont-Cenis Training Center synthesizes many green strategies, as well as pioneering the 'micro-climatic envelope,' whose vast interior shelters a microcosm of urban life. It was built as part of the larger project of regenerating Germany's once mighty industrial Ruhr. The ambitious, Ruhr-wide Emscher Park IBA (International Building Exhibition) is replacing the economically depressed, toxically contaminated legacy of the past with a vision of a verdant future respectful of ecological principles.

The new structure, built where the mine head of the Mont-Cenis coal mine once stood, is used for short residential training courses and also brings employment and civic facilities to the newly amalgamated towns of Herne and Sodingen. These facilities are located in two rows of buildings flanking a tapering central street sheltered within the 123,000 square-foot glass shed. This micro-climatic envelope—a hybrid of greenhouse and Greek temple, combining a high-tech skin with motorized openings (the roof and panes in each wall open automatically in warm weather) and a timber structure whose tree-trunk columns are exposed along an open

front porch—serves several purposes.

Inside, it achieves in northern Europe a Mediterranean climate where an 'outdoor' life can be enjoyed, protected from the rain and cold. The roof and west elevation are covered with 100,000 square feet of photovoltaic cells, which generate two and a half times the energy consumed by the complex. Even without the photovoltaics, however, the strategy achieves considerable economies in energy use. Notwithstanding the vast size of the external envelope in relation to the inner buildings, the Training Center was economical to build. The inner structures do not have to be built to high standards of insulation and weather exclusion, and the envelope itself is clad in the most economical module of single glazing. Materials used are from local sources where possible. The 50-foot high by 16-inch diameter pine trunks used for columns are from nearby forests, as is the wood for the laminated timber trusses and the deciduous wood cladding the inner buildings. The glass is from even closer by, as are the photovoltaic cells, from a factory made viable by this contract and now part of Emscher Park's green future.

1 low energy/ high performance

2 replenishable sources

3 recycling: eliminating waste and pollution

4 embodied energy

5 long life, loose fit

6 total life cycle costing

8 access and urban context

9 health and happiness

10 community and connection

In summer, the glass roof, rows of panes towards the top and bottom of the outer walls, and huge sliding doors in the outer walls, all open automatically (under the control of the building management system linked to sensors) to let cool breezes through. The roof is shaded by the photovoltaic cells and internal, horizontal mesh roller blinds that heat up slightly to aid stack effect ventilation.

When the surrounding park is complete, the glass walls will be shaded in summer by deciduous trees. Standing among the trees are air inlet stacks. Fans suck fresh air from the stacks through tunnels some 10 feet below the ground. There it is cooled by the earth, which remains constant in temperature throughout the year. The air is then drawn into the inner buildings. No air-conditioning is required.

In winter the outer glass skin is sealed, the air inside the envelope is warmed by the sun, and the inner buildings are mechanically ventilated, with the underground tunnels now warming the incoming air. All heat generated inside these buildings is also recaptured from the exhaust air by a heat recovery system and returned to heat the inner buildings. Additional heat and electricity are produced by a co-generation plant that uses methane escaping from the old mine.

This page: The training center is part of a larger redevelopment of what had been the functional center of a mining town. Around the old pit-head where the center now stands is a new park, its landscaping extending inside the glass envelope, and to the east is new housing. Together these bring a vision of a green future to what had been a rust-belt.

Opposite page top: Exterior view.

Bottom: Wood-decked terrace outside cafeteria edges central piazza/street.

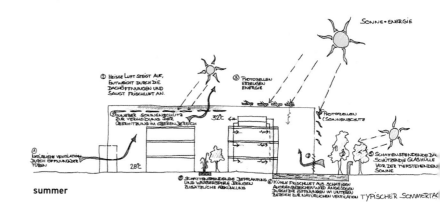

summer

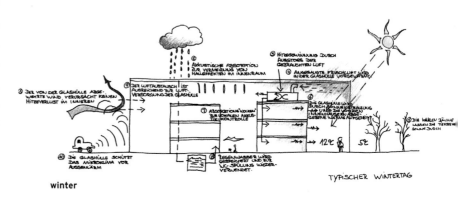

winter

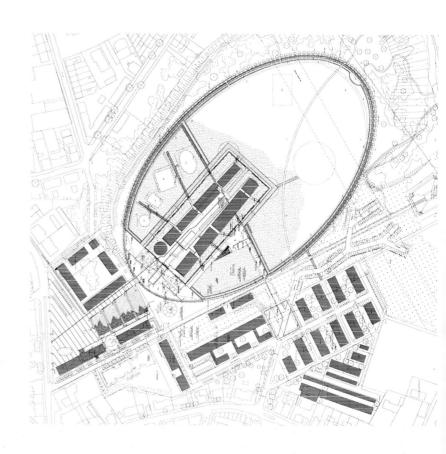

The glass shed is large enough to have its own microclimate, in which a semi-outdoor Mediterranean life style is possible in cold climes. This is enjoyed especially in the tapering plaza-street between academic and residential blocks and on the boarded terrace that overlooks this from outside the cafeteria and multi-purpose hall shared by local community and training center.

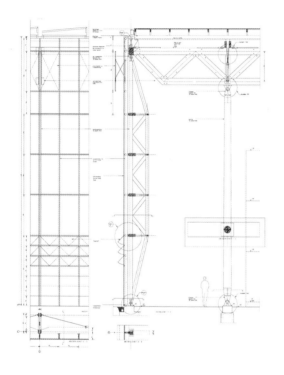

Opposite page: Close-up view of south-west corner of glass outer envelope shows windows open along head of west elevation and photovoltaic cells providing shade as well as electricity on roof. Note also contrast between crisp high-tech minimalism of glass and steel skin and the more rustic and substantially tactile wooden structure with steel joints and ties inside.

This page: Photovoltaic cells on the roof and west facade provide some shade and generate more electricity than the building needs. Internal planting provides further shade and helps modulate the microclimate inside the shed. Projecting shelves reflect light into wood-clad internal academic block.

Climate: Cool Temperate
Edinburgh lies in the northeast of
Britain, with slightly colder
winters and warmer summers than
central England.

Average daily temperature (F):

month	min	max	monthly precipitation
Jan	34	42	2.2
April	39	51	1.5
July	52	65	3.3
Oct	44	54	2.6

Slateford Green

Edinburgh, Scotland 1996-2000
Andrew Lee for Hackland + Dore

A DIVERSE COMMUNITY INHABITS A LOW-RISE, LOW-ENERGY WALL OF HOUSING—AN ADAPTATION OF THE TRADITIONAL TENEMENT—THAT ENFOLDS A MULTI-FUNCTIONING LANDSCAPED COURT DESIGNED FOR BOTH ECOLOGICAL PURPOSES AND TO STIMULATE SOCIAL INTERACTION.

Slateford Green adapts the form of the traditional Edinburgh tenement to wrap a looped wall of 120 apartments around a landscaped court closed at one end by a kindergarten. The complex is green in many ways, not least in sheltering a mixed community that includes families, single and disabled people. It is also well served by buses and adjacent to a proposed commuter station.

To minimize energy consumption the apartments are super-insulated with a material made from recycled newspapers and have conservatories that in winter collect solar heat during the day and are closed off at night by sliding insulated shutters. The common stairwells, like the bathrooms and kitchens, are naturally ventilated using the stack effect. The building materials are low in embodied energy (except for the aluminum roof) and extracted from sustainable or recycled sources with minimum waste, and can themselves be easily recycled. The external walls are constructed from materials that breathe, allowing moisture to escape. This both ensures longer life for the building fabric and more healthy conditions for the occupants. Allowance has been made for retrofitting with

photovoltaic cells to power all external lighting and lighting of common areas inside.

The extensive landscaping uses low-maintenance native species as much as possible and includes ponds surrounded with reed beds to purify rain water runoff from roofs and roads, before this is released into the local stream system. These ponds and reed beds also shelter wild life and form the focal features of the central communal garden. The upper court of the communal garden is paved, and like the gardens which edge it, is designed for use by the disabled who occupy these ground floor apartments. The lower court has a central play space within a grove of native trees. Residual space around the housing wall and the access road that rings it are communal parkland or private allotments.

The development promises to be the frame of a vibrant community life. Immediately at hand are a wide variety of spaces and activities for adults and children, as well as chances to meet, and whether in a private garden or public space, people are visible to and so known to each other in the diverse roles of their daily lives.

1 low energy/ high performance

2 replenishable sources

3 recycling: eliminating waste and pollution

4 embodied energy

5 long life, loose fit

7 embedded in place

8 access and urban context

9 health and happiness

10 community and connection

Slateford Green is designed to engender a richly varied and supportive community life. It mixes different kinds of households and has a range of outdoor spaces suitable for many sorts of outdoor activities while also providing many opportunities for social interaction.

The wall of housing contains a wide variety of unit types. The landscaping, using mainly native species, includes areas of differing character and use: paved areas with raised plant beds for the disabled; playgrounds for children; allotments to grow vegetables; reed beds and ponds to filter and collect water, and shelter wildlife.

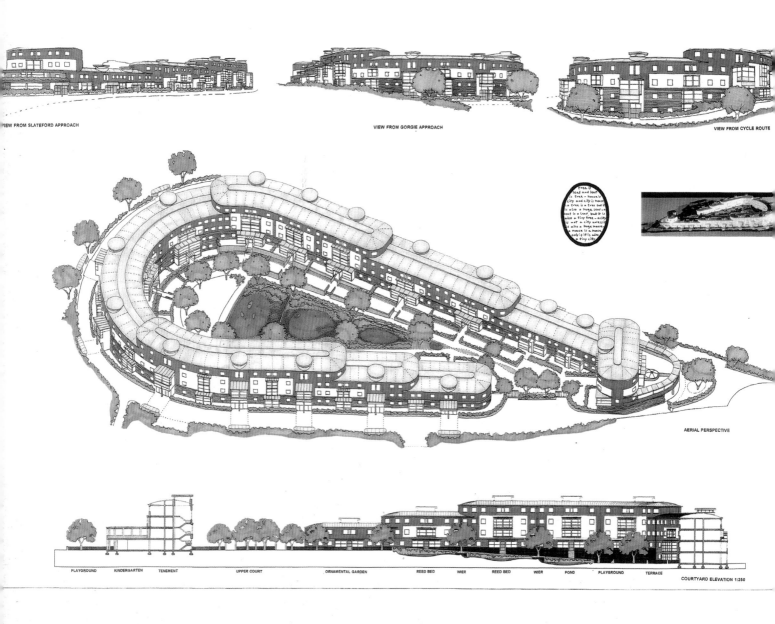

VIEW FROM SLATEFORD APPROACH

VIEW FROM GORGIE APPROACH

VIEW FROM CYCLE ROUTE

AERIAL PERSPECTIVE

PLAYGROUND   KINDERGARTEN   TENEMENT   UPPER COURT   ORNAMENTAL GARDEN   REED BED   WIER   REED BED   WIER   POND   PLAYGROUND   TERRACE

COURTYARD ELEVATION 1:250

Opposite page, top left: Entry to the common stair halls is articulated by projecting porches. Circular lanterns light the stairs and induce stack-effect ventilation. These are designed for retrofitting with photovoltaic cells to generate electricty to light all common areas, outside and inside.

Opposite page, top right and bottom: The wall of apartments enfolds an inner courtyard, the communal focus of the design. To help engender a sense of community, occupants are visible to each other not only when enjoying the different kinds of outdoor activities in the public spaces; they can also be glimpsed, and have contact with the public spaces, when in their private gardens and, if they choose, even in their conservatories.

This page: Design of apartments, common stair halls and courtyard are all considered in terms of energy saving and microclimate.

Construction is as green as possible. Except for the brick-lined stairwells, structure is of local wood: I-sectioned studs and joists engineered for minimal waste. Highly insulated 3-breathing 2-wall construction allows moisture to escape from walls and rooms, ensuring structural longevity and healthy conditions inside. Conservatories capture solar heat in winter.

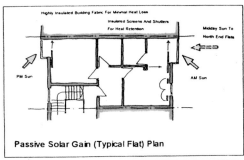

Passive Solar Gain (Typical Flat) Plan

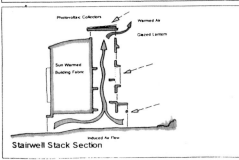

Stairwell Stack Section

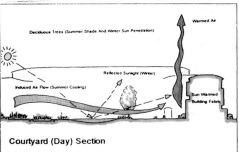

Courtyard (Day) Section

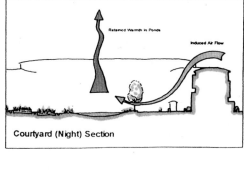

Courtyard (Night) Section

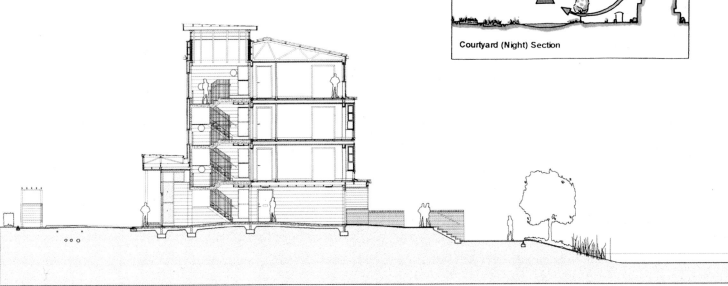

BINSTORE   PORTICO   PEND   CLOSE   GARDEN   LOCHAN POND

Westcott-Lahar House Climate:
Warm Temperate
Bolinas lies on the Pacific Coast,
near San Francisco, with cool to mild
summers and wet winters.

Average daily temperature (F):

month	min	max	monthly precipitation
Jan	45	55	4.7
April	49	62	1.5
July	53	65	0.0
Oct	54	68	1.0

Palmer House Climate:
Desert
Tucson has hot days and cool nights,
with low precipitation year-round.

Average daily temperature (F):

month	min	max	monthly precipitation
Jan	39	65	0.8
April	53	82	0.4
July	77	104	1.0
Oct	56	86	0.4

South Texas Ranch House Climate:
Warm Temperate/Steppe
Cotulla is in the hot arid brush
country of South Texas.

Average daily temperature (F):

month	min	max	monthly precipitation
Jan	36	55	2.5
April	55	75	4.2
July	75	94	2.8
Oct	57	78	2.8

Howard House Climate:
Cold Temperate
Nova Scotia is part of Maritime
Eastern Canada, with temperatures
moderated by the Atlantic Ocean.

Average daily temperature (F):

month	min	max	monthly precipitation
Jan	15	32	5.4
April	31	47	4.5
July	55	74	3.8
Oct	41	57	5.4

1   low energy/ high performance

2   replenishable sources

4   embodied energy

7   embedded in place

Four Houses

Fernau & Hartman Architects
Rick Joy Architect
Lake/Flato Architects
Brian Mackay-Lyons Architecture Urban Design

FOUR HOUSES, EACH FROM A DIFFERENT CLIMATIC REGION OF NORTH
AMERICA, EXTEND THE TRADITION OF A MODERN ARCHITECTURE THAT
DRAWS ON THE FORMS AND MATERIALS OF THE LOCAL VERNACULAR TO
BE CLIMATICALLY APT TO AND SENSITIVELY EMBEDDED IN PLACE.

WESTCOTT/LAHAR HOUSE
West Marin County, California 1996-98
Fernau & Hartman

The Westcott/Lahar House consists of a strip, one room deep, that zig-zags across the upper corner of a large wooded lot on a gentle slope above the Bolinas Lagoon. The thick, well-insulated back wall of the strip is made of straw bales, carved into here and there for punched windows, while the opposite wall is largely glazed and opens to the sun and onto the series of courts the house is folded around. Each court and its adjacent rooms are dedicated to different functions: cooking and eating, living and playing, and sleeping. The resulting composition, that echoes the vernacular of rural north Californian buildings and is eminently suited to its Mediterranean-type climate, nestles cosily into its site and opens up to both the adjacent paved spaces it shelters and more distant views it draws into relationship with itself as it unfolds in a richly experiential and episodic manner.

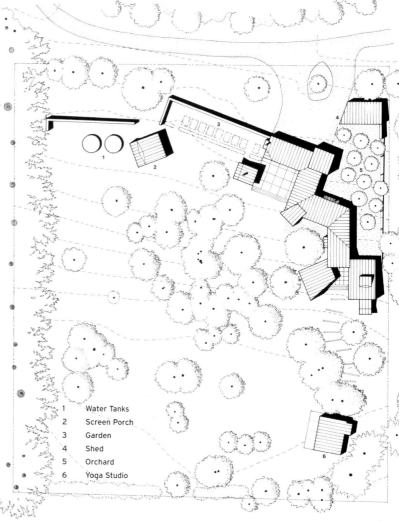

1 Water Tanks
2 Screen Porch
3 Garden
4 Shed
5 Orchard
6 Yoga Studio

0   5   10

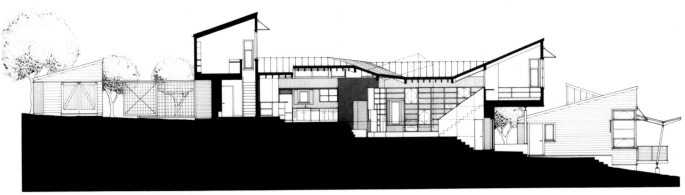

1 Pizza Oven
2 Courtyards
3 Living Room
4 Shed
5 Orchard
6 Kitchen
7 Dining

8 "Elbow" Room
9 Studies
10 Children's Bedrooms
11 Master Bedroom

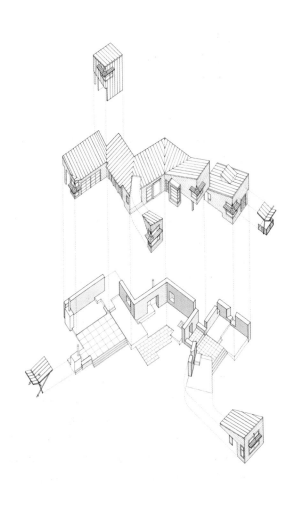

PALMER HOUSE
Tucson, Arizona 1997-98
Rick Joy Architect

The Palmer house, on the edge of a large arroyo north of Tucson, resurrects the traditional massive rammed earth walls of local vernacular and plays these off against thin pre-rusted steel sheets used on roofs and garage walls in a crisply angular composition. The design also preserved all the trees and cacti on the site. Requiring minimal water and maintenance, these grace the courtyard between the garage and the house set towards the northern edge of the site. The house opens up through large stretches of frameless glazing, on the shaded northern side, to uninterrupted views of the Catalina Mountains. Although the thick insulation between steel roof and ceilings of rough-sawn Douglas fir (the same material as the doors) and the high thermal inertia and insulation of the walls do much to keep the house cool and to smooth out diurnal temperature variations, the house is also cooled by an economic evaporative cooling system and heated by a radiant hot water system under the concrete floors. This is a house that combines cool modernity with a sensual, archaic earthiness to be both of its time and very much of its place.

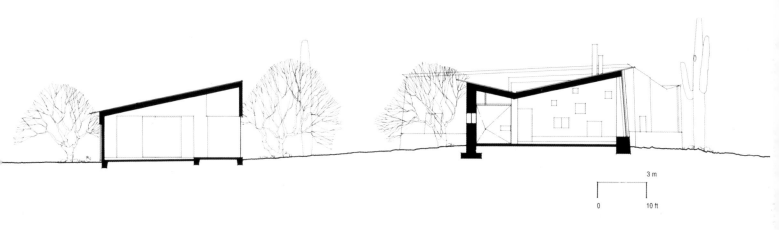

3 m

0   10 ft

1   Entry
2   Living
3   Kitchen
4   Pantry
5   Porch
6   Bedroom
7   Den
8   Spa
9   Garage
10   Guest Bedroom
11   Shop

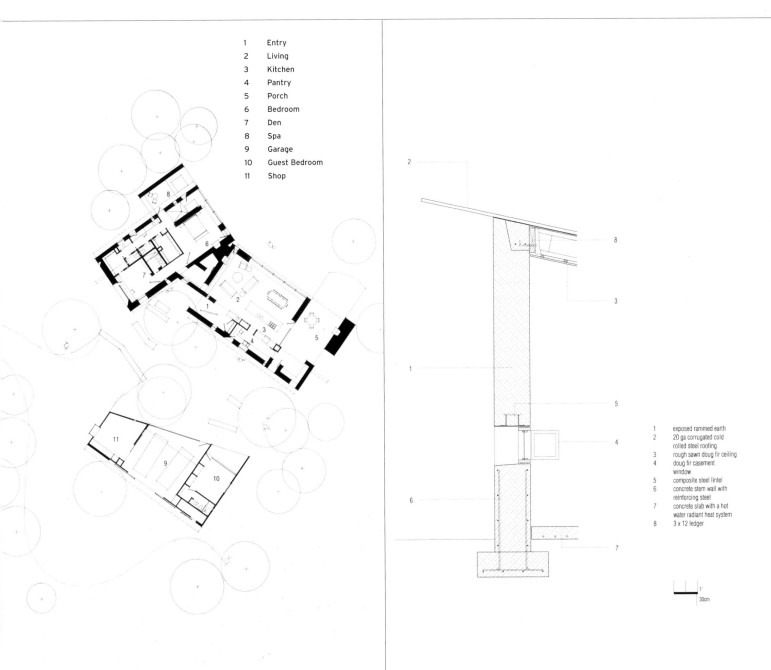

1   exposed rammed earth
2   20 ga corrugated cold
     rolled steel roofing
3   rough sawn doug fir ceiling
4   doug fir casement
     window
5   composite steel lintel
6   concrete stem wall with
     reinforcing steel
7   concrete slab with a hot
     water radiant heat system
8   3 x 12 ledger

1'
30cm

SOUTH TEXAS RANCH HOUSE
Cotulla, La Salle County, Texas 1995-1996
Lake/Flato Architects

The South Texas Ranch House combines two very different elements, an extroverted elliptical pavilion enclosed by heavy buttress-like stone piers, and an introverted patio enclosed at its corners by L-shaped stuccoed blocks. These reflect the contrasting aspects of the site: the lush banks of the Nueces River, which the living and dining pavilion crests, and the arid brush country that stretches away from the bedroom court, a form strongly reminiscent of the patios of the traditional haciendas of this region of Texas. For most of the year the pavilion is enclosed only by mesh screens so as to admit the breezes, which are drawn in also by the air rising under the roof to escape from a central lantern. Only in the short cold season is it necessary to close the glazed shutters, which are usually folded back against the deep piers. The single depth of rooms around the patio and the breezeways between the rooms (through another screened porch on the side opposite the pavilion, a pergola on the otherwise open entrance side and across a large 'stockpond' opposite that) keep the bedrooms well ventilated. Cisterns in the corners of the patio capture precious rainwater. This is a house of many moods and contrasting experiences, that can be lived in in many ways, according to the occupant's mood or the weather.

A   entrance pergola

B   patio

C   living/dining pavilion

D   kitchen

E   bedroom

F   stock pond

G   screened porch

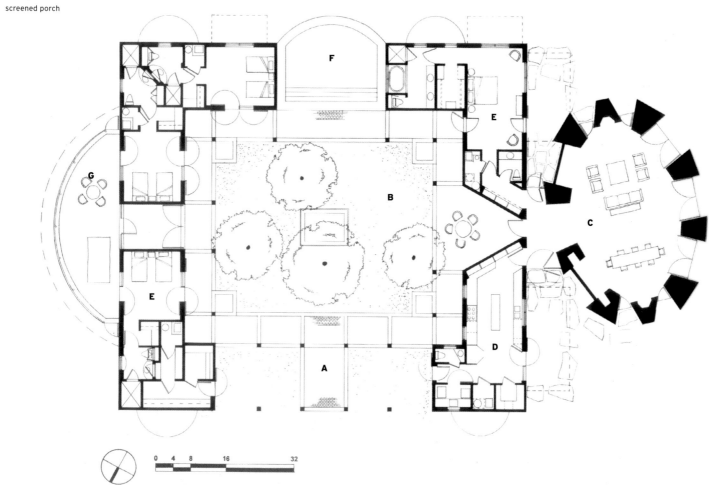

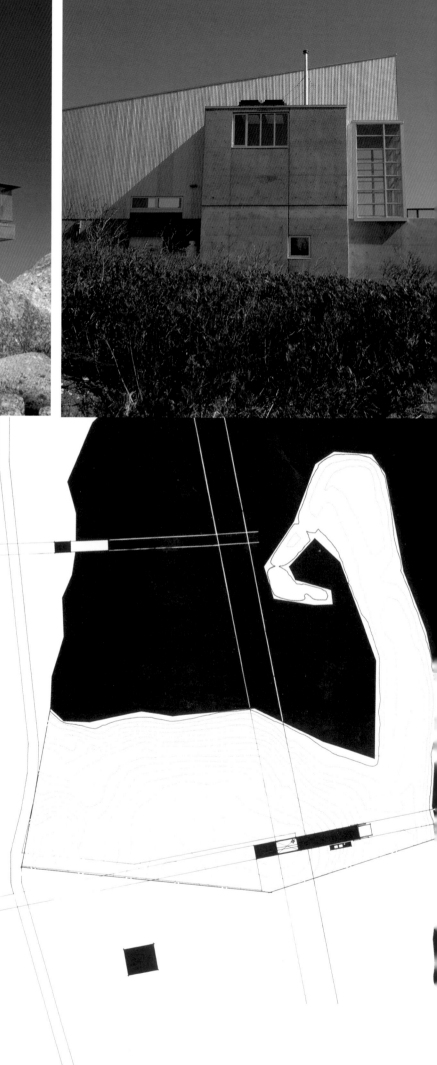

HOWARD HOUSE

West Pennant, Nova Scotia 1995-1998
Brian MacKay-Lyons

Through simple but powerful gestures the Howard House takes possession of a site surrounded on three sides by sea. Set between a calm cove and open ocean, it is a 110 foot long by 12 foot wide wedge that sweeps up in counterpoint to the gentle slope of the site. A large south-facing window and balcony overlook the bay that mediates between the other two contrasting seascapes. A slot through the wedge separates the garage from the house and forms an entrance portico while also establishing a strong cross axis linking cove and ocean. This assertive form clad in unpainted corrugated galvanized steel is inspired by the vernacular, not of cute cottages, but of the local fisheries, boat sheds and barns that show their sensitivity to site by the confidence with which they possess it. This is a vernacular that not only uses wood with a skill informed by the local ship building tradition but uses whatever other materials and standard components are readily available in the most direct of manners.

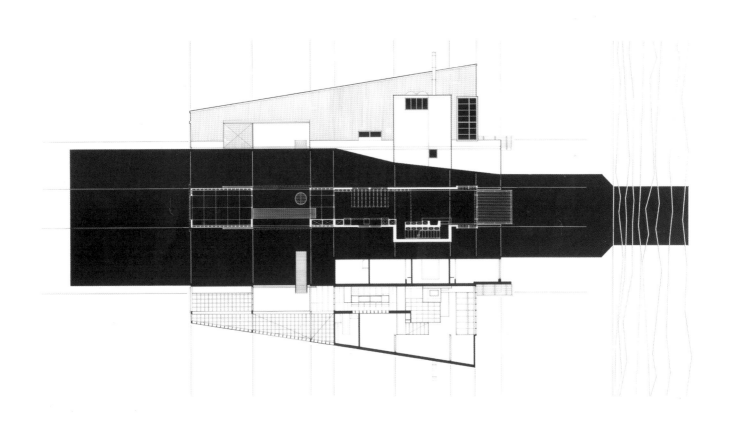

111

Project Credits

BEYELER FOUNDATION MUSEUM
Riehen (Basel), Switzerland
1991-97

Client
Beyeler Foundation

Architect
Renzo Piano Building Workshop
Renzo Piano, Bernard Plattner,
senior partner-in-charge
in association with Burckhardt +
Partner AG, Basel

Preliminary Design, 1992
Design team: Loik Couton (architect
in charge) with P. Hendier,
W. Matthews, R. Self and L.
Epprecht; J. P. Allain (models)

**Design Development and
Construction phase, 1993-1997**
Design team: L. Couton (architect
in charge) with P. Hendier,
W. Matthews, R. Self, and
L. Epprecht; J. P. Allain (models)

Consultants
Structural Engineering
Ove Arup & Partners, C. Burger +
Partner AG

Plumbing
Bogenschütz AG

HVAC
J. Forrer AG

Electrical Engineering
Elektrizitäts AG

Landscaping
J. Wiede, Schönholzer + Stauffer

COMMERZBANK HEADQUARTERS
Frankfurt am Main, Germany
1991-1997

Client
Commerzbank AG

Architect
Foster and Partners, London

Project team: Norman Foster,
Spencer de Grey, Ken
Shuttleworth, Mark Sutcliffe,
Brandon Haw, Robin Partington,
Hans Brouwer, Uwe Nienstedt,
Sven Ollmann, George Brennan,
Stefan Behling, John Silver,
Paul Kalkhoven, Arthur
Branthwaite, Chris Eisner,
Christopher Allercamp, Giuseppe
Boscherini, Simon Bowden,
Thomas Braun, Eckhardt Burling,
Kei-Lu Cheong, Charles Collett,
Penny Collins, Nigel Curry, John
Drew, Matthew Downing, Alex
Gounaris, Nadi Jahangiri, Natalie
Maguire, Nikolai Malsch, Matthias
Massari, Stig Mikkelson, Logan
Reilly, Michael Richter, Giles
Robinson, Cormac Ryan, Thomas
Scheel, Paul Scott, Mandy Bates,
Kinna Stallard, Christine Tonsche,
Huw Turner, Peter Unkrig,
Ken Wai, Andreas Wolff, Alan
Wilkinson-Marten, Louisa
Williams, Michael Wurzel

Consultants

**Structural, traffic, and fire
Engineering**
Ove Arup & Partners with
Krebs & Kiefer

Mechanical Engineering
J. Roger Preston with Petteren &
Ahrens

Electrical Engineering
Schad & Hölzel

Lifts
Jappsen and Stangier

**Project Management/
Construction Management**
Nervus GmbH

Quantity Surveyor
Davis Langdon & Everest

Space planning
Quickborner Team

**Facades, radar, acoustics
and building physics**
Ingenieur Büro Schalm (IBS)

Lighting
Lichtdesign

Landscaping
Sommerlad

Graphic design
Per Arnoldi

COTTON TREE PILOT HOUSING
Queensland, Australia
1992-1994

Client
Department of Public Works and Housing and Chris and Gwen Beecham

Architect
Clare Design
Project Team: Lindsay Clare, Kerry Clare, Jeff Lee, Alan Rogers, Scott Chaseling, Terry Braddock, Troy Zwart

Consultants
Engineering
McWilliam Consultants

Builder
Peter LeCompte

GÖTZ HEADQUARTERS
Würzburg, Germany
1993-1995

Client
Götz GmbH, Metall- u. Anlagenbau

Architects
Webler + Geissler Architekten BDA
Project team: Garnet Geissler, Martin Webler, Markus Greif, Helmut Reifsteck

Consultants
Structural engineering
Ing. Büro Rudi Wolff

Energy Concept
Loren Butt

Energy Management Systems
Marcus Püttmer, Götz GmbH

HALL 26
Hanover, Germany
1994-1996

Client
Deutsche Messe AG, Hannover
Representative of the Board: Sepp D. Heckmann; Technical direction for the central district: Dr. Rainar Herbertz

Architect
Design and planning: Herzog + Partner Architekten BDA, Munich
Concept phase only: Professor Thomas Herzog, Hanns Jörg Schrade with Prof. Michael Volz;

Project architect: Roland Schneider
Assistants: Sabine Erdt, Nico Kienzl, Stefan Öhler, Christian Schätzke, BSrbel Schuster, Thomas Straub, Brigitte Tacke, Stefanie Zierl
Concept phase only: Markus Behr, Hannelore Huber, Anton Pittlinger, Jan Rützel, Rainer Schmid
Realization: BKSP Projektpartner GmbH, Hanover
Manager: Ingo Brosch;
Project architect: Thomas Haase
Assistants: Hans-Joachim Kaub, Joachim Eulig, Bärbel Degner, Martina Elsner, Ulrike Sickau, Klaus Wenzel

Consultants
Structural Engineering
Schlaich Bergermann und Partner, Stuttgart
Prof. Dr. Drs. h.c. Jörg Schlaich

Project partner: Andreas Keil
Project engineer: Frank Simon

Assistants: Frauke Bettermann,
Jochen Bettermann, Hansmartin
Fritz, Ulrich Otto, Peter Scheffold,
Volkwin Schlosser, Renk
Horstmann Renk, Laatzen

Mechanical Services
HL Technik, Munich
Prof. Klaus Daniels

Project engineer: Bernd
Kretschmar
Assistants: Horst-Dieter Recknagel,
Norbert Rosner, Heinz Wese,
Hagen Goletz
With the assistance of (concept
phase only): GfA Gesellschaft für
Aerophysik mbH, Munich,
Bernhard Bauhofer

ETH Eidgensssische Technische
Hochschule Zürich
Institut für Hochbautechnik,
Lehrstuhl für Haustechnik, Ludwig
Ilg Krantz-TKT

Electrical Installation
ROM, Hamburg
Höhne GmbH, Hanover

**Aerodynamic Studies, Natural
Ventilation,
Energy Simulation**
Design Flow Solutions, Arrington,
England,
Dr. Richard A. Waters, Prof. Phil
Jones

Natural and Artificial Lighting
Bartenbach LichtLabor GmbH,
Munich
Prof. Christian Bartenbach

Assistants: Robert Müller, Markus
Platzer, Norbert Reithmaier

Fire Prevention
Hosser, Hass + Partner,
Braunschweig
Dr. Jörn Klaus

Project Management
Assmann Beraten + Planen GmbH,
Braunschweig
Dr. Wolfgang Henning, Horst
Blessmann

**UNIVERSITY OF
NOTTINGHAM
JUBILEE CAMPUS**
Nottingham, England
1996-1999

Client
University of Nottingham

Architect
Michael Hopkins & Partners

Design team: Michael Hopkins,
William Taylor, Bill Dunster, Simon
Fraser, Jan Mackie, Uli Moeller,
Matthew Hoad, Steve Harris,
Rachel Sayers, Eric Svenkerud,
Toki Hoshino, Alex Sykes, Gina
Raimi

Consultants
Structural and Services engineers
Ove Arup & Partners

Landscaping
Battle McCarthy

MINNAERT BUILDING
Utrecht, The Netherlands
1994-1997

Client
University of Utrecht

Architect
Neutelings Riedijk Architecten,
Rotterdam

Design team: Willem Jan
   Neutelings, Michel Riedijk,
   Jonathan Woodroffe, Evert Crols,
   Jago van Bergen, Gerrit Schilder,
   Burton Hamfelt, Chidi Onwuka,
   Joost Mulders

Consultants
Technical Design and Building
Bureau Bouwkunde Rotterdam

Structural Design
ABT Adviesbureau voor
bouwtechniek, Velp

Building Services Engineering
Ingenieursburo Linssen bv,
Amsterdam

Building Physics
Adviesbureau Peutz & Associes bv,
Molenhoek

Interior Design
N.R.A. and F.B.U. (Facility
Management University)

Landscaping
West 8 Landscape Architects bv,
Rotterdam

Artists
Frans Parthesius, Perry Roberts,
Tejo Remy

Builder
Aanneming Maatschappij J.P. van
Eesteren bv, Rotterdam

MONT-CENIS TRAINING CENTER
Herne-Sodingen, Germany
1991-1999

Client
Entwicklungsgesellschaft Mont-
Cenis GmbH, Federal State
Nordrhein-Westfalen, City of Herne,
Internationale Bauausstellung
Emscher Park GmbH, Stadtwerke
Herne AG

Architects
Jourda & Perraudin Architectes
Jourda Architectes, Paris
Hegger Hegger Schleiff, HHS
Planer + Architekten BDA, Kassel

Project architects: Gavin Arnold,
   Lauren Levallois, Tilman Latz

Consultants
Structural engineering
Ove Arup & Partners, Schlaich
Bergermann + Partner, HL
Technik AG

Photovoltaics
Pilkington Solar Inernational GmbH

Glass facade
Gebru. Schneider

Interior design
Jourda Architectes

Landscaping
Desvignes + Dalnaky; Latz, Riehl,
Schulz

Lighting
HL Technik AG

Climate and daylight simulations
Institut für Licht und Bautechnik

Interior wood construction
VHM, Kaufmann

Project management
DMP GmbH

SLATEFORD GREEN MILLENNIUM PROJECT
Edinburgh, Scotland
1996-2000

Client
Canmore Housing Association
Alan Brown (Director), Graham
Harper, Susan Napier, John Lowis
(Clerk of Works)

Architect
Competition Design
Andrew Lee, Bryan Thomas

Site Architects
Hackland + Dore Architects Ltd

Design team: Andrew Lee, project
    architect; Duncan Kidd;
    Irene Barkley; Linda Chiew;
    Alastair Hackland, director-in-
    charge

Consultants

Engineering
Harley Haddow Partnership

Project engineer: Mark Lawler
Assistants: Paul Robertson, John
    Wood, David Robertson

Quantity Surveyor
Summers & Partners
Jim Sneddon, Alan Newlands

Landscaping
RPS Cairns
Emily Peel Yates

Builder
Hart Builders
Colin Jack, contractor manager,
Alex Swanson, site foreman

HOUSES

Palmer House
Tucson, Arizona
1997-1998

Client
John Palmer

Architect
Rick Joy Architect
Design Team: Rick Joy, principal;
Andy Tinucci, Chelsea Grassinger,
Franz Buhler

Consultants
Structural Engineering
M.R. Behnejad, P.E. Southwest
Structural Engineers, Inc.

Mechanical and Plumbing
Roy T. Otterbein, P.E.

Landscaping
Michael Boucher Landscape
Architect

Builder
Rick Joy Architect
Design team: Franz Buhler, Chelsea
    Grassinger, Kevin Stewart, Scott
    Woodward, Matthew Miller,
    Maartje Steenkamp

Construction of rammed earth walls
Quentin Branch, Rammed Earth
Solar Homes, Inc.
Benchmark Concrete, Parsons Steel
Erectors, Romanoski Glass and
Mirror, Lambach Electrical, Bud
Brown Plumbing, Sheet Metal
Flashings, Inc.

Westcott-Lahar House
Bolinas, California
1996-1998

Client
Julie Westcott and David Lahar

Architects
Fernau & Hartman Architects

Partners-in-charge: Richard Fernau,
    Laura Hartman
Project architect: Jeffrey L. Day,
    Alexis Masnik
Design team; Alexis Masnik, Anni
    Tilt, Don Najita and Michael
    Roche, project team; Jeffrey L.
    Day, Alexis Masnik, Sean Gilmore,
    Pietro Calogero
Presentation: Jane Lee

Consultants

Structural Engineering
The Hartwell Company

Mechanical Engineering
William Mah Engineers

Electrical Engineering
Hansen & Slaughter, Inc.

Landscaping
Lizzy Hirsch/Arcadia Garden
Architecture

South Texas Ranch House
La Salle County, Texas
1995-1996

Client
Anonymous

Architect
Lake/Flato Architects
Principal-in-charge: Ted Flato
Project architect: Graham Martin

Consultants
Structural Engineering
Reynolds-Schlattner-Chetter-Roll,
Inc.

Mechanical Engineering
Lozano-Wilson & Associates;
Comfort Air

Howard House
West Pennant, Nova Scotia
1995-1998

Client
Vivian and David Howard

Architect
Brian MacKay-Lyons Architecture
Urban Design
Brian MacKay-Lyons, Niall Savage,
Trevor Davies, Talbot Sweetapple

Consultants
Structural Engineering
Campbell Corneau Engineering
Limited

Builder
Andrew Watts

Photo Credits

Introduction
15   [top] Peter Buchanan
      [middle] Alex Kliment
      [bottom] Peter Buchanan
17   Robert Lautman
20   Foster and Partners Image
      Realization
23   [top left] Richard Schenkirz
      [top right] Dieter Leistner/artur
      [bottom left] Dieter
      Leistner/artur
      [bottom right] Dieter
      Leistner/artur
25   [top left] Nigel Young/Foster
      and Partners
      [top right] Dennis Gilbert
      [middle left] Nigel Young/Foster
      and Partners
      [bottom left] Foster
      and Partners
      [bottom right] Foster
      and Partners
27   [top left] Michael Hopkins
      and Partners
      [top right] Michel Denancé
      [middle left] John Gollings
      [bottom left] Michael Hopkins
      and Partners
      [bottom right] Richard Davies

Beyeler Foundation Museum
      All drawings and plans courtesy of
      Renzo Piano Building Workshop.
40-1   Christian Richters
42   [top] Michel Denancé
43   [top] Michel Denancé
      [middle bottom] Michel Denancé
44   [top left] Michel Denancé
45   [top] Michel Denancé
      [bottom] Christian Richters

Commerzbank
      All drawings and plans courtesy
      of Norman Foster and Partners.
46-7   Ralph Richter/architekturphoto
48   [left] Ian Lambot
      [top right] Ralph
      Richter/architekturphoto
      [bottom right] Ian Lambot
49   [bottom left] Ian Lambot
      [bottom right] Nigel
      Young/Foster and Partners
50   [middle right] Ian Lambot
53   [left] Foster and Partners Image
      Realization

      [bottom right] Ian Lambot
54   [top] Nigel Young/Foster
      and Partners
      [bottom] Ian Lambot
55   [top] Nigel Young/Foster and
      Partners
      [bottom] Ian Lambot

Cotton Tree Housing
      All drawings and plans courtesy
      of Clare Design.
56-7   Richard Stringer
58   Richard Stringer
59   [right] Richard Stringer
61   Richard Stringer

Götz Headquarters
      All drawings and plans courtesy
      of Webler + Geissler.
62-3   R. Halbe/artur
65   Andreas Lauble/Webler +
      Geissler
66   Andreas Lauble/Webler +
      Geissler

Hall 26
      All drawings and plans courtesy
      of Herzog + Partner.
68-9   Dieter Leistner
70   [top] Aerophot-Demus
71   [top] Aerophot-Demus
      [bottom] Dieter Leistner/artur
72   [top left] Roland Schneider
      [top right] Herzog + Partner
      [middle left] Thomas Hasse
      [middle right] Thomas Hasse
      [bottom left] Thomas Hasse
      [bottom right] Frank Simon
      [bottom] Dieter Leistner/artur
73   [bottom] Dieter Leistner/artur

Jubilee Campus, University of Nottingham
      All drawings and plans courtesy
      of Michael Hopkins and Partners.
74-5   Dennis Gilbert
77   University of Nottingham
79   Martine Hamilton Knight
81   [top] Martine Hamilton Knight
      [bottom] Ian Lawson

Minnaert
      All drawings and plans courtesy
      of Neutelings Riedijk Architecten.
84-5   Christian Richters

86   [top] Brakke-Scagliola
      [bottom] Christian Richters
89   [top] H. Van Doorn
      [middle] Christian Richters
      [bottom] H. Van Doorn

Mont-Cenis
      All drawings and plans courtesy
      of Jourda Architectes.
90-91   Paul Raftery
93   [top] Paul Raftery
      [bottom] Paul Raftery
94   [right] Paul Raftery
95   [top] Paul Raftery
      [bottom] Paul Raftery

Slateford Green
      All drawings and plans courtesy
      of Hackland + Dore.
96-7   John Reiach
99   John Reiach
100   John Reiach

Four Houses
102   [top left] Todd Hido
      [top right] James Steeves
      [bottom left] Michael Lyon
      [bottom right] Wayne NT Fuji'l

Westcott/Lahar House
      All drawings and plans courtesy
      of Fernau & Hartman
104   [top] Richard Barnes
105   [top]Todd Hido

Palmer House
      All drawings and plans courtesy
      of Rick Joy Architects.
106   Wayne NT Fuji'l

South Texas Ranch House
      All drawings and plans courtesy
      of Lake/Flato Architects.
108   Michael Lyon
109   Michael Lyon

Howard House
      All drawings and plans courtesy
      of Brian Mackay-Lyons.
110   James Steeves
111   [top left] Undine Prohl
      [top right] James Steeves

Exhibition Credits

Curator:
Peter Buchanan

Project director:
Rosalie Genevro

Exhibition coordinator:
Andrew Blum

Project development:
Gregory Wessner

Exhibition Design:
Lewis. Tsurumaki. Lewis

Print graphics:
Asya Palatova

Introductory text graphics:
Tricia Solsaa

Video editing:
George Ratliff

Computer presentations:
Brian Spinks

Installation support:
Teresa Harris, Anne Rieselbach

Publication coordination:
Andrew Blum, Alex Kliment,
Gregory Wessner

Additional help with graphics
was provided by:
Kimberly Brown, Faye Premer,
Sara Lundgren, Peter Theis,
Eva Tiedemann, and Hans P. Walter

Display Tables Fabrication:
Veyko Design

Photo and Panel printing:
Baboo Color Labs

Projection Screen and Introductory
Panel Fabrication:
Troy Ostrander

Commerzbank model builders:
Gia Wolff, Judith Tse,
Carla Munoz-Puente

University of Nottingham Jubilee
Campus model builders: Brendan
Lee, Emily Abruzzo, Damien
Jackson, Miko Smith, Christine
Kang, Herbin Ng

Hall 26 model builders: Gia Wolff,
Carla Munoz-Puente

Slateford Green model builders:
Brendan Lee, Emily Abruzzo,
Christine Kang

Mount Cenis Training Center
model builders: Emily Abruzzo,
Brendan Lee

Minnaert Building model builder:
Alex Chan

The Architectural League gratefully
acknowledges the assistance of the
following people from architectural and
engineering practices represented in
the exhibition:

BDSP: Klaus Bode, Matthew Kitson

Brian MacKay-Lyons Architecture Urban
Design: Nancy Anningson, Brian
MacKay-Lyons

Clare Design: Kerry and Lindsay Clare

Fernau/Hartman Architects:
Kate Demong, Richard Fernau,
Laura Hartman

Foster and Partners: Stefan Behling,
Katy Harris, Elizabeth Walker

Hackland + Dore: Andrew Lee

Herzog + Partner: Thomas Herzog,
Franziska v. Wedel

Jourda Architectes: Françoise Jourda,
Nicola Kiwall, Tilman Latz

Lake/Flato Architects: Paul Schoenfeld

Michael Hopkins and Partners: Nicky
Dewe, Claire Endicott, Jan Mackie,
Bill Taylor

Neutelings Riedijk Architecten: Daphne
Maaskant, Willem Jan Neutelings

Ove Arup and Partners: John Berry,
Angela Green, Alistair Guthrie,
Andrew Sedgwick, Christian Topp

Renzo Piano Building Workshop:
Giorgio Bianchi, Giovanna Giusto,
Shunji Ishida, Bernard Plattner,
Boris Vapné

Rick Joy Architect: Rick Joy,
Andy Tinucci

Roger Preston and Partners:
Ian Mulquiney

Webler + Geissler Architekten:
Martin Webler.

Exhibit Travel Schedule

Architectural League of New York
The Urban Center
New York City
April-May 2000

College of Architecture,
University of Texas at Austin
University of Texas at Austin
Austin, Texas
September-October 2000

National Building Museum
Washington, D.C.
December 2000-February 2001

College of Architecture,
University of Houston
University of Houston
Houston, Texas
March-April 2001

Committee on the Environment,
Colorado Chapter, AIA
Museum of Contemporary Art
Denver, Colorado
May-June 2001

City of Portland Office of
Sustainable Development
Natural Capital Center
Portland, Oregon
September 2001

Berkeley Art Museum
University of California at Berkeley
Berkeley, California
October-November 2001

Salt Lake City Corporation
Salt Lake City Public Library
Salt Lake City, Utah
January-March 2002

Orange County Museum of Art
Newport Beach, California
April-June 2002

Committee on the Environment,
Boston Chapter, AIA
Boston Architectural Center
Boston, Massachusetts
September-November 2002

Committee on the Environment,
Las Vegas Chapter, AIA
Neonopolis
Las Vegas, Nevada
November 2002-January 2003

School of Architecture,
Washington University
Washington University
St. Louis, Missouri
February-April 2003

Air Pollution Control District,
Louisville, Kentucky
Glassworks Gallery
Louisville, Kentucky
June-September 2003

Architalx
Institute of Contemporary Art
Portland, Maine
November-December 2004

Select Bibliography

New books on green issues, both generally and focusing on the built environment, appear so frequently that any bibliography is soon dated. The following lists are far from comprehensive, but record some titles found useful, enjoyable and inspiring when and since preparing this book and the exhibition on which it is based. The latter part of the list is of books setting a larger framework within which architects may think and design—one far more inspiring and illuminating of the emerging future than most of the theory (critical or otherwise) in which many architects and academics currently indulge.

GREEN BUILDINGS

Behling, Sophia and Stefan, with Bruno Schindler, foreword by Sir Norman Foster. *Solar power : the evolution of solar architecture*. New York: Prestel, 2000.
Packed with images and information, this is a book to be dipped into frequently and should be in the libraries of all architects and architectural students.

Buchanan, Peter. "Steps up the Ladder to a Sustainable Architecture." *A+U* (May 1997): 6-13.
An essay outlining some of the themes that are taken further in this book.

Buchanan, Peter. "Invitation to the Dance: Sustainability and the Expanded Realm of Design." *Harvard Design Magazine* (Spring/Summer 2003).
Written three years after *Ten Shades of Green*, this is an update on the author's thinking in an issue of the magazine devoted to green design.

Cuito, Aurora, ed. *Eco-tecture: Bioclimatic Trends and Landscape Architecture in the Year 2001*. Barcelona: Loft Publications, 2000.
A wide-ranging, if rather arbitrarily selected, collection of buildings and landscaping projects.

Edwards, Brian and Hyett, Paul. *Rough Guide to Sustainability*. London: RIBA Publications, 2001.
Small and useful.

Farmer, John. *Green Shift: Changing Attitudes in Architecture to the Natural World*. Boston: The Architectural Press, 1999.
A survey of the various strands of green thinking that have pervaded modern architecture.

Fernandez-Galiano, Luis. *Fire and Memory*. Translated by Gina Cariño. Cambridge, MA: MIT Press, 2000.
At first glance it looks arcane, but the themes are central to green design.

Herzog, Thomas editor. *Solar Energy in Architecture and Urban Planning*. Munich: Prestel, 2nd edition, 1998.
Packed with examples, but like all such books too sketchily presented for in-depth study.

Jones, David Lloyd. *Architecture and the Built Environment: Bioclimatic Building Design*. Woodstock, New York: Overlook Press, 1998.
An international collection of green buildings with informative introductory chapters. Still one of the best of its sort.

Kibert, Charles J., Jan Sendzimir and G. Bradley Guy, eds. *Construction Ecology: Nature as the basis for green buildings*. London: SPON Press, 2002.

Melet, Ed. *Sustainable Architecture: Towards a Diverse Built Environment*. Rotterdam: NAI Publishers, 1999.

Scott, Andrew, ed. *Dimensions of Sustainability: Architecture, Form, Technology, Environment, Culture.* London/New York: E & FN Spon, 1998.
Transcripts from a conference. Some useful articles, but needed the attention of an editor.

Van der Ryn, Sim, and Stuart Cowan. *Ecological design.* Washington, D.C.: Island Press, 1996.
Tends to the rough-hewn, low-tech end of green design that puts off some architects but offers many sound and widely applicable concepts.

Wines, James. *Green Architecture.* Cologne/New York: Taschen, 2000.
A lavishly illustrated and wide-ranging book that might be light on rigor and technical discussion—tending to show designs that look green, and are often more so in spirit than in performance—but is a readily available and appealing introduction to the subject.

Zelov, Chris, and Phil Cousineau, eds. *Design Outlaws on the Ecological Frontier.* Philadelphia: Knossus Publishing, 1997.

There are numerous monographs on the more established architects whose works are shown in this book, including the four volumes of the *Renzo Piano Building Workshop: Complete Works* by Peter Buchanan and published by Phaidon Press and *Thomas Herzog: Architecture + Technology*, which includes an introductory essay by Peter Buchanan and is published by Prestel.

GREEN CITIES, SETTLEMENTS, AND LANDSCAPES

Andruss, Van, Christopher Plant, Judith Plant, and Eleanor Wright, eds. *Home! A Bioregional Reader.* Philadelphia, PA: New Society Pubs., 1990.
Contains many useful essays on and around an important subject.

Beatley, Timothy. *Green Urbanism: Learning From European Cities.* Washington, D.C.: Island Press, 2000.
A broad and informative survey of what is being achieved in Europe.

Birkland, Janis. *Design for Sustainability: a Sourcebook of Integrated Eco-Logical Solutions.* London: Earthscan Publications Ltd, 2002.
Packed with ideas and information, user friendly and immensely useful. Should be in every architect's library.

Buchanan, Peter. "Gomera Regional Planning Study". *Norman Foster Works 1.* Munich: Prestel, 2002, 180-191.
Early (1975) study of application of green principles at regional scale.

Girardet, Herbert. *Cities, People, Planet: Livable Cities for a Sustainable World.* Chichester, England: Wiley-Academy, 2004.

Manzini, Ezio and Francois Jegou. *Sustainable Everyday: Scenarios of Urban Life.* Milan: Edizione Ambiente, 2003.

McHarg, Ian L. *Design with Nature.* New York: J. Wiley, 1992.
The classic that initiated green design disciplines. Still vitally relevant.

Myers, Norman. *The Gaia Atlas of Future Worlds: Challenge and Opportunity in a World of Change.* London: Gaia Books, 1990.

Ravetz, Joe. *City-Region 2020: Integrated Planning for a Sustainable Environment.* London: Earthscan Publications Ltd, 2000.

Register, Richard. *Ecocities: Building Cities in Balance with Nature.* Berkeley: Berkeley Hills Books, 2002.

Rogers, Richard, with Philip Gumuchdjian, ed. *Cities for a Small Planet.* London: Faber and Faber, 1997.
A pithy introduction to the subject.

Rogers, Richard, with Anne Power. *Cities for a Small Country.* London: Faber and Faber, 2000.

Rudlin, David, and Nicholas Falk. *Building the 21st Century Home: The Sustainable Urban Neighbourhood.* Oxford: Architectural Press, 1999.
Wide-ranging introduction to sustainable urbanism.

Wackernagel, Mathis, and William Rees. *Our Ecological Footprint: Reducing Human Impact on the Earth.* New catalyst bioregional series, no. 9. Philadelphia, PA: New Society Publishers, 1996.
The concept of the ecological footprint gives a vivid picture of how unsustainable a particular city or town is. This is an excellent, user-friendly introduction to understanding and measuring ecological footprints, a discipline that will
be considered of vital importance, and widely applied in the near future.

GREEN PRODUCTS AND PROCESSES

Datschefski, Edwin. *The Total Beauty of Sustainable Products.* Crans-Pres-Celigny: RotoVision SA, 2001.
Cleverly conceived and attractively presented.

McDonough, William, and Michael Braungart. *Cradle to Cradle: Remaking the Way We Make Things.* New York: North Point Press, 2002.

Wann, David. *Deep Design: Pathways to a Livable Future.* Washington: Island Press, 1996.
A wide-ranging book that should be read by all environmental and product designers.

GREEN ISSUES GENERALLY

Abram, David. *The Spell of the Sensuous: Perception and Language in a More-than-Human World.* New York: Pantheon Books, 1996.

Ausubel, Ken. *Restoring the Earth: Visionary Solutions from the Bioneers.* Tiburon, California: H J Kramer, 1997.
A collection of essays that should inspire optimistic action by showing a range of ways in which green issues are being tackled.

Berry, Thomas. *The Great Work: Our Way Into the Future.* New York: Bell Tower Press, 1999.
An inspiring discussion of the great cultural project of our times: the necessary changes to our ways of thinking and living to ensure our survival and a more noble and satisfying way of being on the earth. See also: Berry, Thomas. *The Dream of the Earth.* San Francisco, California: Sierra Club Books, 1988.

Bruges, James. *The Little Earth Book.* Alistair Sawday Publishing, Expanded 3rd edition, 2002.
A cheap and small-format, yet very wide-ranging and reader-friendly, introduction to the environmental crisis.

Burne, David. *Get a Grip on Ecology.* London: Weidenfeld & Nicholson, 1999.
Although the design and brown paper pages may be a bit off-putting, this is a very accessible introduction to the subject.

Capra, Fritjof. *The Hidden Connections: A Science of Sustainable Living.* London: Harper Collins, 2002.

Clinebell, Howard. *Ecotherapy: Healing Ourselves, Healing the Earth.* New York: Haworth Press, 1996.

Goldsmith, Edward. *The Way: An Ecological Worldview.* Boston: Shambhala, 1993.

Gore, Albert. *Earth in the Balance: Ecology and the Human Spirit.* Boston: Houghton Mifflin Co., 2000.

Hartmann, Thom. *The Last Hours of Ancient Sunlight: Waking up to Personal and Global Transformation*. New York: Harmony Books, 1999.
A powerful analysis of the environmental crisis and the cultural dynamics of the long process by which it came about, as well as provocative proposals for its solution.

Hawken, Paul, Amory B. Lovins and L. Hunter Lovins. *Natural Capitalism: The Next Industrial Revolution*. London: Earthscan Publications, 1999.

Jensen, Derrick. *Listening to the Land: Conversations About Nature, Culture, and Eros*. San Francisco: Sierra Club Books, 1995.
Interviews with 29 different thinkers giving very different perspectives on environmental issues.

Korten, David C. *The Post-Corporate World: Life After Capitalism*. San Francisco and West Hartford: Berrett-Koehler Publishers and Kumarian Press, 1999.
One of the best discussions of the economic changes necessary to achieve sustainability. See also Hartmann, Thom. *Unequal Protection: The Rise of Corporate Dominance and the Theft of Human Rights*. Rodale Inc., 2002

Lynas, Mark. *High Tide: News from a Warming World*. London, Flamingo, 2004.

Mau, Bruce, with Jennifer Leonard and Institute without Boundaries. *Massive Change*. London: Phaidon, 2004.

Ponting, Clive. *A Green History of the World: The Environment and the Collapse of Great Civilizations*. London: Sinclair-Stevenson Ltd., 1991.

Roszak, Theodore. *The Voice of the Earth*. New York: Simon & Schuster, 1992.

Speth, James Gustave. *Red Sky at Morning: America and the Crisis of the Global Environment*. New Haven: Yale University Press, 2004.

Schor, Juliet B, and Betsy Taylor, eds. *Sustainable Planet: Solutions for the Twenty-first Century*. Boston: Beacon Press, 2002.
Essays on wide range of approaches to sustainability

Spowers, Rory. *Rising Tides: The History and Future of the Environmental Movement*. Edinburgh: Canongate Books Ltd, 2002.

Spretnak, Charlene. *The Resurgence of the Real: Body, Nature, and Place in a Hypermodern World*. Reading, Massachusetts: Addison-Wesley, 1997.

Weizsacker, Ernst U. von, Amory B. Lovins, and L. Hunter Lovins. *Factor Four: Doubling Wealth—Halving Resource Use: The New Report to the Club of Rome*. London: Earthscan Publications Ltd, 1997.
The key book on how vastly improved resource efficiency can bring a better, greener future for all.

Acknowledgements

For help in preparing and researching this book and the exhibition it documents, I am most grateful for the help I received from a number of people.

Most especially I want to thank and acknowledge for their time and input, and also for their unflaggingly cooperative attitude and good humor: Rosalie Genevro, Executive Director of the Architectural League of New York, who commissioned and managed the production of the exhibition and book; her husband Armand LeGardeur, for all the weekends and evenings he babysat and was without his wife who was working with me; and David Lewis, Marc Tsurumaki and Paul Lewis of Lewis.Tsurumaki.Lewis, the architects who designed the exhibition.

I am also most grateful to Asya Palatova for her splendid design of this book; to Andrew Blum for obtaining and coordinating all the material for the show and book; and to Alex Kliment and Gregory Wessner who tied up the loose ends of acquiring materials for the book. From the architects included I thank: Bill Taylor and (especially for showing me around the Jubilee Campus and all her subsequent help) Jan Mackie of Michael Hopkins and Partners: Stefan Behling (for his advice) and Katy Harris of Foster and Partners; Thomas Herzog of Herzog and Partner, for showing me his buildings at the Hanover Fair grounds; Françoise Jourda and Tilman Latz of Françoise Jourda Architectes; and Giorgio Bianchi of Renzo Building Workshop. Many thanks also to Sinisa Stankowic and Klaus Bode of mechanical engineers BDSP for showing and explaining to me some of their work and for the extracts of animated computer modelling that are included in the exhibition.

- PETER BUCHANAN

PETER BUCHANAN

Born in Malawi and schooled in Zimbabwe, Peter Buchanan studied architecture at the University of Cape Town, graduating in 1968. He has worked as an architect, urban designer and planner in various parts of Africa, Europe and the Middle East. He is also a writer and critic, curator and consultant. Through the 1980s he was Deputy Editor of *The Architectural Review*, publishing prolifically in that journal and others. Since 1992 he has freelanced: curating exhibitions (including *Renzo Piano Building Workshop: selected projects* and *Ten Shades of Green* – both were initiated by the Architectural League of New York and have toured widely), writing the four volumes of *Renzo Piano Building Workshop: Complete Works* and *Ten Shades of Green*, and consulting on urban design and green issues. His interest in the latter originates from his early years in practice in Cape Town, before he moved to London in 1972 where he still resides.

KENNETH FRAMPTON

Kenneth Frampton is Ware Professor of Architecture at Columbia University.

ROSALIE GENEVRO

Rosalie Genevro is Executive Director of the Architectural League.

The Architectural League of New York

The Architectural League of New York is an independent forum for the presentation and discussion of creative and intellectual work in architecture, urbanism, and related design disciplines. Founded in 1881, the League promotes excellence and innovation in architecture and urbanism by furthering the education of architects and designers, and by communicating to a broad audience the importance of architecture in public life. Through an active schedule of programs, the League provides a venue for contemporary work and ideas, identifies and encourages the work of talented young architects, creates opportunities for exploring new approaches to problems in the built environment, and fosters a stimulating community for dialogue and debate. All of the League's work is shaped by its ongoing commitment to interdisciplinary, intergenerational, and international exchange, and by its concern for the quality of architecture and city form as critical components of a vital and dynamic culture.

The Architectural League of New York
457 Madison Avenue
New York, NY 10022
www.archleague.org